REFLECT...

by
Burns K. Seeley, Ph.D.

Nihil Obstat: Rev. John A. Hardon, S.J.
Censor Deputatus
Imprimatur: Rev. Msgr. John F. Donoghue
Vicar General of the Archdiocese of Washington, D.C.
April 20, 1982

Library of Congress Card Number 82-072202

ISBN Number 0-932406-07-6

Item number for this book is 323-78
The Apostolate, Box 220, Kenosha, WI 53141

Copyright MCMLXXXII The Apostolate for
Family Consecration, Inc.

File in
The Apostolate's Prayerbook
Book A4-1, Behind Section 2, Chapter 111

or

Living Meditation and Prayerbook Series
Book A4-3, Behind Section C2, Chapter 103

Structured by Jerome F. Coniker
Edited by Dale Francis

Full color cover picture and halftone meditation pictures copyright 1955 through 1963 The Apostleship of Prayer, used by permission.

Information coding from the Coniker Communications System, copyright 1977, 1978 and 1980 Coniker Systems, Inc. used by permission.

Excerpts from The Jerusalem Bible copyright 1966 by Darton Longman & Todd, Ltd. and Doubleday and Company, Inc., used by permission of the publisher.

Copyright MCMLXXXII The Apostolate for Family Consecration, Inc.

Published by
Apostolate for Family Consecration
The Apostolate, Box 220
Kenosha, Wisconsin 53141

International Center
Arlington, Virginia

Printed in U.S.A.

*This book and the entire
Reflections on St. Paul
Peace of Heart Forums
are dedicated to the
Holy Face of Jesus
for the renewal of family life
throughout the world.*

Table of Contents

Prayers 1
Introduction 7
Four C's Reflections on St. Paul

First Week Day 1 (Colossians 1:1-2:23) 37
First Week Day 2 (Colossians 3:1-4:18) 48
First Week Day 3 (I Thessalonians 1:1-2:20) . 57
First Week Day 4 (I Thessalonians 3:1-5:28) . 66
First Week Day 5 (2 Thessalonians 1:1-3:18) .. 77
First Week Day 6 (I Timothy 1:1-2:15) 87
First Week Day 7 (I Timothy 3:1-4:16) 96

Second Week Day 1 (I Timothy 5:1-25) 105
Second Week Day 2 (I Timothy 6:1-21) 114
Second Week Day 3 (2 Timothy 1:1-18) 124
Second Week Day 4 (2 Timothy 2:1-26) 133
Second Week Day 5 (2 Timothy 3:1-4:22) .. 142
Second Week Day 6 (Titus 1:1-16) 152
Second Week Day 7 (Titus 2:1-3:15) 159

Third Week Day 1 (Philemon 1-25) 168
Third Week Day 2 (Hebrews 1:1-3:19) 175
Third Week Day 3 (Hebrews 4:1-5:14) 187
Third Week Day 4 (Hebrews 6:1-8:13) 196
Third Week Day 5 (Hebrews 9:1-10:39) 208
Third Week Day 6 (Hebrews 11:1-40) 220
Third Week Day 7 (Hebrews 12:1-13:25) ... 229

Scripture References 241

The Work and Goals of the Apostolate 245

The Litany of the Sacred Heart of Jesus ... 254

The Litany of Our Lady of Loreto 258

The Litany of St. Joseph 262

The Chaplet of the Divine Mercy 265

Act of Consecration

Heavenly Father, grant that we, who are nourished by the Body and Blood of Your Divine Son, may die to our own selfishness and be one spirit with Christ, as we seek to fulfill Your distinctive plan for our lives.

Form me and all the members of my family, community, and the Apostolate into instruments of atonement. Unite our entire lives with the Holy Sacrifice of Jesus in the Mass of Calvary, and accept our seed sacrifice offering of all of our spiritual and material possessions, for the Sacred and Eucharistic Heart of Jesus, through the Sorrowful and Immaculate Heart of Mary, in union with St. Joseph.

Our Father, let Sacred Scripture's Four "C's" of Confidence, Conscience, seed-Charity, and Constancy be our guide for living our consecration as peaceful children and purified instruments of the Most Holy Family.

Let us live our consecration by remaining perpetually confident, calm, cheerful, and compassionate, especially with the members of our own family and community.

Please protect our loved ones and ourselves from the temptations of the world, the flesh and the devil. Help us to become more sensitive to the inspirations of Your Holy Spirit, the Holy Family, our Patron Saints and Guardian Angels.

And now, Most Heavenly Father, inspire us to establish the right priorities for Your precious gift of time. And most of all, help us to be more sensitive to the needs and feelings of our loved ones.

Never let us forget the souls in Purgatory who are dependent upon us for help. Enable us to gain for the Poor Souls of our loved ones and others, as many indulgences as possible. We ask You this, Our Father, in the name of Our Lord and Savior Jesus Christ, Your Son and the Son of Mary. Amen.

Cenacle Prayer

(To Be Recited Before All AFC Gatherings)

Our Father, we gather together in the Name of Your Son Jesus Christ, and ask You to cast out all demons coming against our families and the Apostolate for Family Consecration.

We entrust this gathering to the Sorrowful and Immaculate Heart of Mary, in union with St. Joseph. And through the intercession of our Patrons, especially that of St. Vincent Pallotti, the Patron of all lay apostolates, we ask You to enable us, personally and collectively, to fulfill Your distinctive plan for our lives.

Father, we offer You the Precious Body, Blood, Soul and Divinity of Your Son, Our Lord Jesus Christ, in atonement for all of our sins and the sins of our families, neighborhoods, country and the entire world.

Most Holy Spirit, inspire, and protect us from pride, error and division. Bless our Holy Father the Pope, our Bishops and Priests. Also bless the activities and members of the Apostolate in this area.

Most Sacred and Eucharistic Heart of Jesus, pour Your Precious Blood down upon our families and the universal work of the Apostolate for Family Consecration. We particularly pray for the petitions placed at the foot of the Altar in our Sacred Hearts Chapel at the House of St. Joseph.

We ask all of this in Your Name, through the Immaculate Heart of our Mother Mary, in union with the Head of the Holy Family, St. Joseph. Amen.

Seed-Charity Prayer in the Spirit of St. Francis

Lord, make me an instrument of your peace;
Where there is hatred, let me sow seeds of love;
Where there is injury, let me sow seeds of pardon;
Where there is discord, let me sow seeds of union;
Where there is doubt, let me sow seeds of faith;
Where there is despair, let me sow seeds of hope;
Where there is darkness, let me sow seeds of light;
And where there is sadness, let me sow seeds of joy.
O Divine Master, grant that I may not so much seek to be consoled as to console You in others;
To be loved, as to love You in others;
For it is in *giving that we receive.*
It is in pardoning that we are pardoned,
And it is in *dying as a seed to our selfishness that we are born to eternal life.*

Prayer to St. Joseph for The Apostolate

St. Joseph, place me in the presence of the Blessed Sacrament of the altar in the Sacred Hearts Chapel at the House of St. Joseph and unite my prayers with those of the other members and friends of the society of the Apostolate for Family Consecration throughout the world.

We know, St. Joseph, that Our Lord will refuse you nothing. Please ask God to bless the Apostolate and all of its members and friends. Ask Our Lord to help the Apostolate accomplish its goal of establishing an international network of permanent chapters of dedicated volunteers. Ask Jesus to use these chapters to transform neighborhoods into God-centered communities by thoroughly educating people in the spiritual life.

St. Joseph, we are confident that you will remove all obstacles in the path of this spiritual renewal program, so that our society will be transformed through a chain reaction that will renew the family, the neighborhood, the school and the Church.

Form the society of the Apostolate for Family Consecration into a useful instrument of the Holy Family, and never let its members and leaders falsely judge others or fall into the sin of pride or complacency in success, which is so fatal to the work of God. Use the Apostolate as an instrument to bring about the social reign of the Sacred Heart of Jesus and the Immaculate Heart of Mary in our age. Amen.

Come Holy Spirit

Come, Holy Spirit, Who resides in the innermost recesses of my soul and give me the light of Your wisdom through the fire of Your divine love.

INTRODUCTION TO REFLECTIONS ON ST. PAUL

1. Before you begin meditating on St. Paul's letters, please take time to read these introductory pages. They will help you cultivate the art of meditation.

2. When meditating on St. Paul or on other portions of Scripture, we want you to discover for yourselves Scripture's Four C's Formula for Peaceful Seed Living. It is a formula which will enable you to rise above your problems and accomplish worthy goals you never thought possible. It will also enable you to help countless suffering souls on earth and in Purgatory. Therefore, we are first

going to spend a few minutes discussing this formula, concentrating on the nature of each of the Four C's.

3. Then, we will share with you some suggestions on how to meditate well. This will be followed by some background material on St. Paul and his letters, which will help you better understand the man and the message he conveys as Christ's Apostle.

Scripture's Four C's

4. What are Scripture's Four C's? Those of you who are already acquainted with the work of the Apostolate for Family Consecration will no doubt already know the answer, especially if you have read Volume I of our two volume work called "Scripture's Four C's Formula for Peaceful Seed Living" and our "Prayers and Recommended Practices book." *(For information on the work and goals of the Apostolate see pp. 245)*

5. Confidence, Conscience, seed-Charity and Constancy. These are the four pillars of the *Peaceful Seed-Living Formula*. And, we hope the Four C's will become a permanent part of your lives so you will always have ready access to that God-given peace which defies complete understanding.

Confidence (C-1)

6. The first C - "Confidence." When we speak of "Confidence," what do we mean? We mean a supernaturally-given trust in God, a trust in His unique plan for each of us, and a trust in the strength He will give us to

accomplish this plan. Since God is completely good, He desires only what is best for us, namely, our interior peace. But if we are to obtain this inner peace of heart, our trust or confidence must be focused on Him.

7. We also mean by confidence, a supernaturally-given ability to believe the truths which the Father has revealed for our salvation through the patriarchs, the prophets, the Apostles, and especially through Jesus. When we use confidence to mean this type of belief, we are using it in the same way that "faith" is used in most of the New Testament, that is, in the exclusively Christian part of the Bible.

8. Less frequently, we use confidence to mean hope, that is, hope in eternal life with God, hope in the rewards that accompany eternal life and hope in the means of obtaining it.

9. It can be seen then, that we use confidence as a synonym for trust, faith and hope, which are special graces mentioned often in the New Testament and given by God for our salvation.

10. To sum up, The Apostolate speaks of confidence as trust in God, belief in His supernaturally revealed truths, hope in eternal life, and hope in the means to obtain it.

Conscience (C-2)

11. Now, the second C - "Conscience." As used by the Apostolate for Family Consecra-

tion, conscience means a pure conscience, or one that is free from all fully deliberate sins, since these are the major obstacles to spiritual growth and a life of union or oneness with God.

12. Imperfections and half deliberate sins, on the other hand, while they do not prevent us from enjoying God's friendship and a pure conscience, are nonetheless obstacles to obtaining a purer conscience, and can therefore be sources of spiritual illnesses leading to mortal sins. Consequently, we should, with the aid of God's grace, seek to remove them, too, along with all willfull sins.

13. Throughout Scripture, we are commanded to purify our consciences by repenting of our sins so we can grow in holiness and in God's friendship. In order to accomplish this properly, a daily in-depth self-examination for these hindrances to holiness should be undertaken.

Seed-Charity (C-3)

14. Next, our third C - "seed-Charity." Seed-charity or seed-sacrifice, or we could say seed-love, is that grace referred to in the Bible which makes it possible for us to offer ourselves fully to the true service of God and our fellow man. Put another way, we could say seed-charity enables us to love God as He commanded us to do with all our hearts, with all our souls, with all our minds, and with all our strength, and to love our neighbor as ourselves. Indeed, seed-charity enables us to love others as Christ has loved us, that is, even to the point of death.

15. We of The Apostolate prefer the term "seed-charity" to simply "charity" or "love," since in modern English it is not always clear what these latter two terms mean. Thus when we prefix "seed" to charity, we wish to convey the idea of a love which is essentially sacrificial. Without this prefix, charity is often thought of solely in terms of donating time or money to some worthy cause. But activity of this sort is not always sacrificial. Also, the word "love" without the prefix "seed" could mean either romantic love or the love of casual friendship, but neither of these needs to be sacrificial either.

16. If we were to reflect on it, we would all realize a seed is meant to sacrifice itself, or die, so a new life, that of a plant, might slowly emerge and eventually achieve full growth. Similarly, one who exercises sacrificial love or seed-charity dies to his selfishness, so a new

Christ-like individual can emerge and ultimately attain full growth in sanctity through a transforming union with Our Lord.

17. We do not have to look further than our own immediate environment to know where we should plant our seeds of sacrificial charity. And in doing so, we are faithfully fulfilling our responsibilities in our state in life. Trials, for instance, which come upon all of us, can be sanctified by offering them to God in the spirit of seed-charity. When we plant seeds of sacrifice to meet our spiritual needs in this life, we are preparing ourselves for eternal life with God in His heavenly Kingdom. We are also achieving *peaceful seed-living* on earth, and we are having our material and emotional needs met as well.

Constancy (C-4)

18. Finally, the fourth C - "Constancy." By constancy we mean a special supernatural grace which allows us to persevere with a pure conscience in the Christian life, even during moments of difficult temptations. We need this grace to persevere in all acts which lead to our destiny in Heaven, but especially in the exercise of confidence and seed-charity.

19. Constancy is continual living in God's presence. It is a constant vigilance always to do the things that please God. This includes maintaining a positive attitude of expectation for God's love, for responses to our prayers, and for God's harvest from the charitable seeds we have planted. In a certain sense we cay say constancy is the most important of all virtues, since it undergirds and reinforces all the others. Without it, all of our efforts would bear little spiritual fruit.

The Four C's

20. Now let's condense and simplify our definitions of the Four C's. Confidence refers to those graces which make it possible for us to trust and hope in God, and also to believe all the truths He has revealed supernaturally for our salvation.

21. By conscience, we normally mean a conscience which is pure or free of all fully deliberate sins and which is aware of one's faults to be overcome.

22. Seed-charity is the supernatural ability to sacrifice ourselves for God by loving Him

directly through prayer and worship, and also in our neighbor. We love God too by fulfilling our responsibilities and changing our trials into positive seeds of sacrifice.

23. Finally, there is constancy which is a special God-given aid that helps us persevere in the fulfillment of our Christian responsibilities and be alert to God's harvest sent our way to fulfill our needs so we can do His will on earth and finally obtain Heaven.

Meditation

24. Making good meditations is crucial for proper spiritual development. That is why they are an integral part of the Apostolate's spiritual leadership programs.

25. In general, we could say that a spiritual meditation consists simply in making a prayerful reflection on some spiritual topic or topics with the purpose of knowing and loving God better.

26. Sacred Scripture or, for that matter, any number of excellent spiritual books can serve as focal points for meditating since they are rich sources of spiritual subject matter. We would recommend first and foremost, however, the use of Sacred Scripture, inasmuch as it is the primary source book of Christian spirituality.

27. Over the centuries, the Church has highly recommended scriptural meditation. The Second Vatican Council (1962-1965), for example, spoke of scriptural meditation as a means of dialoguing with God. Thus it noted that we speak to God when we pray and we listen to Him when we read (and meditate on) His written Word. *("Dogmatic Constitution on Divine Revelation," #25.)*

28. What are the main steps in a scriptural meditation? First, a quiet place should be found — ideally in a church in the presence of the Blessed Sacrament. But, for many, this may not be practical on a regular basis. Consequently, you might choose an isolated area in your home, such as a bedroom.

29. It would be helpful to start your meditation with a prayer to Mary, the Spouse of the Holy Spirit, for assistance in making your meditation fruitful. And if you have not already done so, it would be well to examine your conscience and confess your sins so there will be no obstacles to the action of God's grace within you. One more thing — it is best to meditate at the same time each day. This makes it easier for meditation to become a habit and, therefore, a normal part of your life.

30. Now, placing the Scripture reading you are going to meditate on in front of you, you should be ready to begin. It is best to read slowly and deliberately, and if you feel moved to do so, to pause from time to time, to reflect on the sentences or passage just read.

31. What do they mean? What is God saying to you and to your families through them? What acts of charity do they suggest? Perhaps they suggest more fervent prayers, or greater generosity to those closest to you, or some special act of seed-charity for someone you have wrongfully injured.

32. Also when meditating try to find within the Scripture readings, words and ideas which suggest the Four C's. You will probably be surprised to see how often they occur. Confidence, as we have already mentioned, can be seen in words such as "faith," "hope" and "trust." Conscience, or a pure conscience, is suggested immediately by terms such as a "pure heart," and an "honest

and good heart." And it is suggested indirectly by many references to sins which must be repented of before a pure conscience can be secured. The idea of seed-charity is found especially in the frequent use of "love" — and the concept of constancy can be found in the use of words such as "persevere" and "endure."

33. Note also in the margins of your Scripture readings, the numbered C's. C-1 represents confidence. C-2 stands for conscience. C-3 stands for seed-charity, C-4 represents constancy, and C-5 represents a combination of the Four C's. These are guides for you in discovering the Four C's in the adjacent Scripture passages. You will undoubtedly discover other references to them as well.

34. It is important that your meditations be forms of prayer, and the subject matter of each prayer should be whatever the Holy Spirit suggests to you while meditating. Perhaps you will be led to express sorrow for your sins or gratitude for having a loving God Who was willing to become man to suffer and die for each of us. Or reflecting on Scripture may bring to mind those who could use your prayers and other sacrificial acts.

35. During the three weeks of the present spiritual formation program, when you have completed your daily meditation on Scripture, read the prepared companion meditation in the same slow, deliberate manner. This is found immediately following the Scripture reading.

36. The purpose of using the companion meditations is to give you additional insights into the meaning of God's written word for yourself, your family and others.

37. We suggest that if you have not meditated regularly before that, at first, you spend only fifteen to twenty minutes a day in tion. Then we recommend you work your way up to a half hour and then perhaps to an hour, both of which will quite likely seem to pass rather quickly. Set your own pace and ask Mary, the Spouse of the Holy Spirit, to take you by the hand and lead you into the spiritual life.

St. Paul

38. Now we would like to acquaint you with St. Paul and his letters. Especially with the eight you will be meditating on for the next twenty-one days.

39. St. Paul was a contemporary of the other Apostles, although not initually one of

them. He was born outside of Palestine in the Jewish section of Tarsus, the capital city of the Roman province of Cilicia, which is now a part of modern Turkey. His Jewish name was Saul, after the first king of Israel. Paul, a Roman name, was given him, some believe, because of his Roman citizenship.

40. St. Paul's early formal education seems to have been exclusively Jewish, and more particularly, Pharisaic; the Pharisees being a Jewish sect favoring the strict observance of the Jewish or Mosiac Law. Although reared as an observant Jew, we should not conclude, therefore, that St. Paul was ignorant of the pagan learning and culture which flourished in his native Tarsus, since echoes of it are found in his writings. This knowledge would later prove helpful in his efforts to convert the pagans to Christianity.

41. In his youth, Paul spoke two languages, Aramaic and Greek. Aramaic, spoken also by Jesus, was the first language of the more conservative Jews in and around the eastern Mediterranean region. Greek was the

language used in the local synagogues and by Paul in his New Testament writings. Later, when he received more advanced education in Jerusalem, Paul learned Hebrew as well. Here, he studied under the famous Gamaliel, a highly respected rabbi and Pharisee. Under Gamaliel's direction, St. Paul mastered Jewish lore, including distinctively Jewish methods of argumentation, which he would later use as a Christian in attempts at converting his fellow Jews.

42. As a Pharisee and rabbi, Paul labored strenuously for the integrity of traditional Jewish doctrine and for the strict observance of the Law of Moses. Moreover, he supported himself, both as a Pharisaic Jew and later as a Christian, not by performing religious duties, but by his hands as a textile worker engaged in making of tents.

43. When Jesus had ascended into Heaven, and the Apostles, recently filled with the power of the Holy Spirit, were beginning to spread the Gospel throughout the world, Paul, or Saul, was still a practicing Pharisaic Jew. As a matter of fact, he regarded the first Christians as followers of a false messiah and a genuine threat to the Mosaic Law. Thus, he zealously sought to persecute them, as we learn from the Acts of the Apostles.

44. "Meanwhile Saul was still breathing threats to slaughter the Lord's disciples. He had gone to the high priest and asked for letters addressed to the synagogues in Damascus, that they would authorize him to

arrest and to take to Jerusalem any followers of the Way (i.e., followers of Christ), men or women, that he could find." (Acts 9:1-2)

45. It was on his way to Damascus, on fire with hatred for Christianity, that his unparalleled conversion experience occurred. On the outskirts of the city, he encountered a vision of the Risen Lord, Who said, "Saul, Saul, why are you persecuting me?... I am Jesus and you are persecuting me. Get up now and go to the city and you will be told what to do." (Acts 9:4-6) Saul then fell to the ground and was blinded for three days. Arriving in Damascus, he was sought out by a Jewish Christian named Ananias. Ananias was told by Our Lord in a vision to find Paul, since, said Jesus, "this man is my chosen instrument to bring my name before pagans and pagan kings and before the people of Israel; I myself will show him how much he must suffer for my name." (Acts 9:15-16)

46. As an Apostle, St. Paul spent the rest of his life tirelessly spreading the Gospel and administering the sacraments among both Jews and Gentiles in the Roman Empire. Continuously suffering in the service of Our Lord and His Church, St. Paul's life ended in martyrdom in Rome about A.D. 67.

The Letters

47. In common with pagan letters of that period, all but one of St. Paul's letters contains an introductory paragraph which includes the name of the writer, the name of the individual or individuals to whom it was written and also a word of greeting. The main body of his letters contains the principal message, with a concluding paragraph containing a farewell and messages from friends.

48. In place of the standard pagan greeting of "health," however, St. Paul normally uses, "grace and peace," and in two of his letters, "mercy." In his concluding paragraphs, he changes the pagan "farewell" for a variation of "the grace of our Lord Jesus Christ be with you."

49. In most of St. Paul's letters, the main body has two sections: the first dealing with doctrinal matters and his relations with those to whom he is writing and the second section pertains to practical problems which he was asked to resolve.

50. Normally, St. Paul dictated his letters,

and would sometimes add a sentence or two at the end in his own handwriting. But, as in the case of his Letter to Philemon, he would on occasion write an entire letter himself.

51. As mentioned earlier, all of St. Paul's New Testament letters were written in Greek, but not the Greek used by the more learned of the day. Rather, it more closely resembled the ordinary spoken Greek.

52. The doctrine found in the letters was derived, in part, from divine revelation given directly to St. Paul. Principally, it came from the following sources: personal contact with the Apostles and disciples of Our Lord, who were with Him while He was on earth; reflection on the Old Testament in the light of Christian revelation; and from his vast knowledge of Jewish teaching. For us, however, who now read St. Paul, everything he wrote was divinely inspired and is, therefore, God's revelation.

53. Now, let's look at a brief overview of each of the eight Pauline letters included in this spiritual growth program.

Colossians

54. This letter is addressed to the Christians who lived in Colossae, a small town located in the southwestern part of the Roman province of Phrygia in what is now modern Turkey. While there were some Jews among its population, most of its inhabitants were pagans. And it is from these pagans that most of the converts to Christianity came.

55. St. Paul, himself, did not personally found the Church in Colossae. Rather, this was principally the accomplishment of Epaphras, Paul's friend and quite likely his disciple.

56. The Letter to the Colossians was written while Paul was in prison in Rome. Its purpose was to strengthen and instruct the new converts in the Catholic Faith.

57. In it, Paul teaches that Christ is the Head of all creation, as well as the Head of the Church and Savior of the human race. St. Paul also declares that he is the servant of both God and the Colossians, thus imitating Our Lord, Who came not to be served but to serve.

58. As the Colossians' true servant, having their best interests at heart, St. Paul warns them against false teaching which threatens their spiritual well-being. He also cautioned them to avoid immoral behavior, noting that it angers God. Then the Apostle gives some general rules about leading Christian lives within a family setting.

1 and 2 Thessalonians

59. The city of Thessalonika, located in the Roman province of Macedonia, was strategically situated on the Via Egnatia, an important military and commercial highway linking the Aegean and the Adriatic seas. The city's harbor was generally regarded as the best in the province. Today Thessalonika is the modern Greek city of Salonika.

60. The Thessalonian Christians generally came from the pagan majority, and not, in this instance, from the large and influential Jewish minority.

61. In I Thessalonians, St. Paul stresses the virtues of faith, patience, and holy living. He addresses himself also the inevitable difficulties that all Christians must face.

62. The main theme of the letter, however, concerns itself with the Second Coming of Christ at the end of the world. And St. Paul stresses the need for constant preparation for its arrival, which will occur unexpectedly.

63. In 2 Thessalonians, St. Paul once more deals with the Second Coming. Moreover, there is also an account of a certain disciple of satan who will precede Christ's return and lead many from the path of salvation.

64. St. Paul warns too against idleness, encouraging the Thessalonians to work and to persevere in the Faith and in virtuous living.

I Timothy

65. St. Paul's First Letter to St. Timothy is one of several letters commonly referred to as the Pastoral Letters or Epistles. They are so-named because they deal largely with practical matters regarding the pastoral care of local Churches.

66. St. Timothy was the disciple and loyal companion of St. Paul. He had a Greek pagan father and a Jewish mother, and seems to have been converted by St. Paul during St. Paul's first missionary journey.

67. In I Timothy, St. Paul counsels his faithful disciple on how to govern, teach and minister to the local Church which was entrusted to his care. Paul writes, for example, that the wealthy are obligated to share their riches with the needy. He also instructs Timothy on certain aspects of Christian widowhood and on how to select worthy clergy to assist him in his numerous responsibilities as chief pastor.

II Timothy

68. Of all St. Paul's known letters, his Second Letter to Timothy is the most personal. In it, St. Paul cautions Timothy to keep and teach, with the aid of the Holy Spirit, the Faith which Paul had entrusted to him. St. Timothy is also given directions on how to endure hardships with the strength that comes from the Lord Jesus Christ. Here St. Paul compares a good Christian to a disciplined soldier, to an athlete and to an industrious farmer. St. Paul deals too with the problem of false teachers who were plaguing the Church at Ephesus with alarming statements such as the claim that the bodily resurrection of mankind from the dead, destined for the end of the world, had already occurred.

69. St. Paul discussed as well the dangers of the last days on earth when evil in families and elsewhere will be rampant. Then, St. Timothy is given a solemn charge to preach the Gospel whether it is welcomed or not. Moreover, he is to refute doctrinal errors and to call the rebellious to obedience.

70. On a personal note, Paul speaks of his impending death, and calls attention to those who deserted him. Yet, following the example of the dying Christ, he expresses the desire that God will not hold them accountable.

Letter to Titus

71. Like the letters to St. Timothy, this one too is a pastoral work in which St. Paul gives practical advice and instructions for the proper administration of a local Church.

72. Titus, himself, is referred to by Paul as a "beloved son." Born of Greek parents, he was destined to become Paul's convert and disciple who would eventually become the bishop of the Mediterranean island of Crete.

73. He was sent at least twice by St. Paul on important missions to Corinth, and during St. Paul's final imprisonment in Rome, St. Titus was sent to Dalmatia. According to tradition, after St. Paul's death, he returned to Crete.

74. In the Letter to Titus, St. Paul describes the qualifications of elders, or priests, who are to be chosen to govern the Church in Crete. They must, for example, be "moral, devout and self-controlled," (Titus 1:8) and well-versed in the unchanging Faith of the Church. As in the case of Timothy, St. Paul warns Titus against false teachers who corrupt the Faith committed by Christ to His Church through the endeavors of the Apostles. Moreover, the faithful are to be taught to be obedient to civil officials and governments.

75. Titus is also given some specific moral instructions. Paul writes, for instance, that the older men are to be "sound in faith and love and constancy" (Titus 2:1) and younger women are to be "sensible and chaste." (Titus 2:5) In essence, St. Paul teaches that everything that does not lead to God must be forsaken.

76. In closing, Titus is encouraged to teach his people in such a way that not only will their faith be strengthened but they will also be induced to constantly perform good works.

Letter to Philemon

77. Philemon, a prominent Gentile Christian of Colossae, was converted through the efforts of St. Paul. His slave, Onesimus, escaped and fled to Rome, where he encountered St. Paul. St. Paul was also responsible for Onesimus' conversion and persuaded him to return to his master. Philemon, himself, was a man of wealth and was noted for helping the poor, as well as for his hospitality, zeal, and loyalty to St. Paul.

78. The Letter to Philemon is also included among Paul's Pastoral Letters. The purpose in writing it was to seek Philemon's forgiveness for Onesimus who had not only run away but seems also to have stolen from his master.

79. At first glance, it may appear that St. Paul approved of slavery, but careful examination of the letter does not produce

irrefutable evidence to this effect. He does, however, tolerate the system, yet not without teaching the principle of the brotherhood of all men in Christ, the acceptance of which would lead to the eventual abolition of slavery.

80. The Letter to Philemon, containing only twenty-five verses, is one of the shortest of the New Testament writings. In summary, we can say the letter is an appeal by St. Paul to the charity of Philemon to be gentle with Onesimus.

Letter to the Hebrews

81. The final letter you will be meditating on is the one addressed simply to "The Hebrews." Written for Jewish Christians, St. Paul sought to strengthen them in their faith and to demonstrate that Christianity is indeed superior to the religion of the Old Testament. *(This letter has been traditionally attributed to St. Paul, although throughout the centuries many scholars have disputed this, largely due to vocabulary and stylistic differences when compared with the more commonly accepted letters of St. Paul. The doctrinal content, however, has Pauline characteristics.)*

82. St. Paul begins the letter by noting that God spoke in the past through prophets, but now He speaks through His own divine Son, Who upholds the entire universe and destroyed the curse of sin.

83. Paul then exhorts the Hebrews to recall frequently the fundamental truths of the Catholic Faith and reminds them it is Christ

alone Who is Savior and Ruler of the universe, to Whom even the angels are subject. The next several chapters deal with Christ as the perfect and merciful High Priest, Who is vastly superior to the high priests and priests of the Old Testament era.

84. "Since in Jesus, the Son of God," said St. Paul, "we have the supreme high priest who has gone through to the highest heaven, we must never let go of the faith that we have professed." (Hebrews 4:14)

85. And since Jesus is the supreme High Priest, St. Paul argues that Christian worship and the intercessory power of Christ are superior to the worship of sacrifices in the Old Testament period. It is also pointed out that, in contrast to the short-lived effectiveness of the animal sacrifices of the Old Testament, it is Jesus' own sacrifice of Himself, involving the shedding of His Most Precious Blood, which instituted an unending covenant with God.

86. Several chapters follow which stress the importance of having a constant faith in God, which endures through all sufferings and trials. St. Paul writes, for example, that "you will need endurance to do God's will and gain what he has promised." (Hebrews 10:36) He insists too that the Hebrews must remain faithful until their souls are saved forever. (Hebrews 10:39). Then, St. Paul presents a long list of Old Testament figures who displayed exemplary faith in God the Father. Next, the author insists that for Christians

Christ must be their constant point of reference since He leads them in their faith and brings it to perfection. (Hebrews 12:3)

87. Finally, the Hebrews are told to be obedient to their religious shepherds. These in turn are accountable to God for the way in which they care for their flocks.

88. As you prayerfully reflect on these eight letters during the next three weeks, we wish you God's blessing and an abundance of spiritual fruit.

"Peaceful Seed Living" Prayer and Meditation Book, Volume II

89. At the end of each of the companion meditations, which follow the daily Scripture selections, note the references to Volume II of the *Peaceful Seed Living* prayer and meditation book. Be sure to read them. These will give you further insights into the spirituality of the Apostolate for Family Consecration, including the spirituality of consecration and of Scripture's Four C's. You will also receive information about the structure of the Apostolate. This small book features Mother Teresa of Calcutta's own meditations and Father John A. Hardon's theological talk on Scripture's Four C's spirituality.

"The Catholic Catechism"
by Fr. John A. Hardon, S.J.

90. You will find many references throughout the following "companion meditations" to Father John A. Hardon, S.J.'s, "The Catholic Catechism," published by Doubleday and Co., N.Y. This handbook on our Faith is one of the most thorough and concise books of its kind. If you want to get the most out of your meditations, we strongly recommend that you obtain a copy of this book and use it during your meditation periods. As Scripture unfolds our Faith, Father Hardon's "Catholic Catechism" will help clarify it for you. If you wish, you may order a copy from the Apostolate, Box 220, Kenosha, WI 53141.

"Modern Catholic Dictionary"
by Fr. John A. Hardon, S.J.

91. Also referred to in the companion meditations are topics defined in Fr. Hardon's *"Modern Catholic Dictionary,"* which is also published by Doubleday & Co. This scholarly work serves as well as a handy reference book featuring thousands of short, easy-to-read, entries on religious topics, including those widely mentioned and discussed since the Second Vatican Council. This, too, can be purchased from the Apostolate.

"The Question and Answer Catholic Catechism"
by Fr. John A. Hardon, S.J.

92. Another book by Father Hardon which

we strongly recommend for parents to use with their children is "The Question and Answer Catholic Catechism," also published by Doubleday and Co. Completely orthodox and up-to-date, this work is written in the catechetical format familiar to many in parishes and Catholic schools some years ago. One advantage of this catechism over some of the earlier question and answer books is the more complete answers given to the questions. "The Catholic Catechism" and the "Modern Catholic Dictionary" can also be used with this book for supplemental information. "The Question and Answer Catholic Catechism" is available as well from the Apostolate.

Neighborhood Peace of Heart Forums

93. While this book on St. Paul's letters can be read as a complete unit in itself, it was primarily designed to be a meditation book for one of the Apostolate for Family Consecration's Neighborhood Peace of Heart Forums. Forums conducted by authorized Neighborhood Chapters of the Apostolate. A Peace of Heart Forum consists of four meetings, over a 22-day period, in private homes for small gatherings of neighbors who come together to view the Apostolate's home video tape television programs and participate in discussing the spiritual truths they have read about and meditated on.

94. If you would like to attend a Neighborhood Peace of Heart Forum or help form a

Neighborhood Chapter in your area, please contact us at the AFC, Box 220, Kenosha, WI 53141.

Purpose of the Apostolate

95. The specific purpose of the Apostolate is to utilize programs, of which this book is a part, to transform neighborhoods into God-centered communities, communities supportive of the sacredness of family life. *(See pages 245-253 for further information.)*

WEEK 1 DAY 1
Colossians 1:1-2:23

Colossians

THE LETTER OF PAUL TO THE CHURCH AT COLOSSAE

PREFACE

Address

1 From Paul, appointed by God to be an apostle of Christ Jesus, and from our 2 brother Timothy ·to the saints in Colossae, our faithful brothers in Christ: Grace and peace to you from God our Father. (C1) (C2)

Thanksgiving and prayer

3 We have never failed to remember you in our prayers and to give thanks for you to God, the Father of our Lord Jesus Christ, 4 ever since we heard about your faith in Christ Jesus and the love that you show toward all 5 the saints ·because of the hope which is stored up for you in heaven. It is only re- (C3) (C3) (C1) (C3) (C1)

cently that you heard of this, when it was announced in the message of the truth. The 6 Good News ·which has reached you is spreading all over the world and producing the same results as it has among you ever since the day when you heard about God's grace and understood what this really is. 7 Epaphras, who taught you, is one of our closest fellow workers and a faithful deputy for

8 us as Christ's servant, •and it was he who told us all about your love in the Spirit.

9 That will explain why, ever since the day he told us, we have never failed to pray for you, and what we ask God is that through perfect wisdom and spiritual understanding you should reach the fullest knowledge of his will. 10 •So you will be able to lead the kind of life which the Lord expects of you, a life acceptable to him in all its aspects; showing the results in all the good actions you do and 11 increasing your knowledge of God. •You will have in you the strength, based on his own glorious power, never to give in, but to bear 12 anything joyfully, •thanking the Father who has made it possible for you to join the saints and with them to inherit the light.

13 Because that is what he has done: he has taken us out of the power of darkness and created a place for us in the kingdom of the 14 Son that he loves, •and in him, we gain our freedom, the forgiveness of our sins.

I. FORMAL INSTRUCTION

Christ is the head of all creation

15 He is the image of the unseen God
and the first-born of all creation,
16 for in him were created
all things in heaven and on earth:
everything visible and everything invisible,
Thrones, Dominations, Sovereignties, Powers—
all things were created through him and for him.
17 Before anything was created, he existed,
and he holds all things in unity.
18 Now the Church is his body,
he is its head.

As he is the Beginning,
he was first to be born from the dead,
so that he should be first in every way;
19 because God wanted all perfection

to be found in him
20 and all things to be reconciled through him and for him,
everything in heaven and everything on earth,
when he made peace
by his death on the cross.

The Colossians have their share in salvation

21 Not long ago, you were foreigners and (C2)
enemies, in the way that you used to think
22 and the evil things that you did; ·but now he (C2)
has reconciled you, by his death and in that
mortal body. Now you are able to appear
23 before him holy, pure and blameless—·as (C2)
long as you persevere and stand firm on the (C4)
solid base of the faith, never letting your- (C1)
selves drift away from the hope promised by (C2)
the Good News, which you have heard, (C1)
which has been preached to the whole human (C5)
race, and of which I, Paul, have become the
servant.

Paul's labors in the service of the pagans

24 It makes me happy to suffer for you, as I am suffering now, and in my own body to do what I can to make up all that has still to be undergone by Christ for the sake of his body, 25 the Church. ·I became the servant of the Church when God made me responsible for 26 delivering God's message to you, ·the message which was a mystery hidden for generations and centuries and has now been re- 27 vealed to his saints. ·It was God's purpose to reveal it to them and to show all the rich glory of this mystery to pagans. The mystery is Christ among you, your hope of glory: 28 this is the Christ we proclaim, this is the wisdom in which we thoroughly train everyone and instruct everyone, to make them all 29 perfect in Christ. ·It is for this I struggle wearily on, helped only by his power driving me irresistibly.

Paul's concern for the Colossians' faith

1 2 Yes, I want you to know that I do have to struggle hard for you, and for those in Laodicea, and for so many others who have 2 never seen me face to face. ·It is all to bind

you together in love and to stir your minds, so that your understanding may come to full development, until you really know God's
3 secret ·in which all the jewels of wisdom and knowledge are hidden.

4 I say this to make sure that no one deceives
5 you with specious arguments. ·I may be absent in body, but in spirit I am there among you, delighted to find you all in harmony and to see how firm your faith in Christ is.

II. A WARNING AGAINST SOME ERRORS

Live according to the true faith in Christ, not according to false teaching

6 You must live your whole life according to the Christ you have received—Jesus the
7 Lord; ·you must be rooted in him and built on him and held firm by the faith you have been taught, and full of thanksgiving.
8 Make sure that no one traps you and deprives you of your freedom by some secondhand, empty, rational philosophy based on the principles of this world instead of on Christ.

Christ alone is the true head of men and angels

9 In his body lives the fullness of divinity, and in him you too find your own fulfillment,

10 in the one who is the head of every Sovereignty and Power.*a*
11 In him you have been circumcised, with a circumcision not performed by human hand, but by the complete stripping of your body of flesh. This is circumcision according to
12 Christ. ·You have been buried with him, when you were baptized; and by baptism, too, you have been raised up with him through your belief in the power of God who raised
13 him from the dead. ·You were dead, because

you were sinners and had not been circumcised: he[b] has brought you to life with him, he has forgiven us all our sins.

14 He has overridden the Law, and canceled every record of the debt that we had to pay; he has done away with it by nailing it to the
15 cross;[c] and so he got rid of the Sovereignties and the Powers, and paraded them in public, behind him in his triumphal procession.[d]

Against the false asceticism based on "the principles of this world"

16 From now onward, never let anyone else decide what you should eat or drink, or whether you are to observe annual festivals,
17 New Moons or sabbaths. ·These were only pale reflections of what was coming: the real-
18 ity is Christ. ·Do not be taken in by people who like groveling to angels and worshiping them; people like that are always going on about some vision they have had, inflating themselves to a false importance with their
19 worldly outlook. ·A man of this sort is not united to the head, and it is the head that adds strength and holds the whole body together, with all its joints and sinews—and this is the only way in which it can reach its full growth in God.

20 If you have really died with Christ to the principles of this world, why do you still let rules dictate to you, as though you were still
21 living in the world? ·"It is forbidden to pick up this, it is forbidden to taste that, it is for-
22 bidden to touch something else"; ·all these prohibitions are only concerned with things that perish by their very use—an example of
23 *human doctrines and regulations!*[e] ·It may be argued that true wisdom is to be found in these, with their self-imposed devotions,

their self-abasement, and their severe treatment of the body; but once the flesh starts to protest, they are no use at all.

42

Week 1 Day 1
Four C's Reflections
on Colossians 1:1-2:23

1. Jesus, as we begin to meditate on this series of letters by St. Paul, guide our thoughts and desires through the action of God the Holy Spirit. May He enlighten our minds and inspire our wills so that our thoughts, words and deeds will be pleasing to You. *(Be sure to read the introductory remarks about St. Paul, his letters, and his Letter to the Colossians in particular beginning on P. 18 of this book.)*

2. Lord, in the first chapter of his Letter to the Colossians, St. Paul refers to the prayers he made on behalf of others.[1] Elsewhere, he wrote that all Christians should pray for one another. They should, he said, never tire of praying for "the saints," i.e., for their fellow Christians.[2] *(The word "saint" did not yet refer exclusively to those in the state of glory in Heaven.)*

3. Most Sacred Heart of Jesus, taking St. Paul as our guide, inspire us to pray often for those in need, especially for our fellow Christians. Actually, Lord, when, as Your instruments, we pray for others, not only do they benefit, but so do we, since we gain merit in Your eyes and we grow in holiness.

4. Constantly remind us also that the help we render others through prayers cannot be duplicated by those who do not pray. When we pray, we become channels of Your supernatural love (seed-charity) aiding souls in ways that mere humanitarians and well-wishers can never do.

5. Jesus, St. Paul reminded the Colossians that they, as Christians, were able to appear before You as holy, pure and blameless, as long as they persevered "on the solid basis of the faith."[3] Thus, continuance in sanctity is based on the on-going acceptance of You as Savior, and all You teach us through Your Catholic Church. Sanctity, however, is not dependent only on the acceptance of the Faith, but also by performing deeds of seed-charity. Moreover, acts of faith and seed-charity must be performed on a continuing basis for us to increase in holiness and remain in the state of grace. *(For a definition of the state of grace, see p. 519 of Father Hardon's "Modern Catholic Dictionary.")*

6. Through Your Church, Lord, You teach us that the great enemy of continued growth in sanctity is mortal sin, since it causes us to lose the gift of seed-charity and sometimes

faith (and hope) as well. But venial sins also should be avoided as much as possible because they tend to weaken our resolve to resist temptations to mortal sin and hinder our growth in holiness. *(For a discussion of mortal and venial sins read pp. 293-295 of Father Hardon's, "The Catholic Catechism.")*

7. Lord, inspire and strengthen us with Your many graces so that we may remain constantly in Your friendship. Especially, may we be both afraid and ashamed to offend You through mortal sin, which causes us to lose our friendship with You and our accessibility to eternal happiness.

8. Jesus, St. Paul reminded the Colossians that he struggled "wearily on,"[4] being aided only by Your power. He said the purpose of his relentless struggle was to make people perfect in Christ.[5]

9. St. Paul's persistence in charity for all never ceases to amaze us, Lord. Following his example, may we also desire the salvation and sanctification of everyone we meet. But

especially may we seek to further the salvation and sanctification of the members of our own families.

10. Jesus, Our King, St. Paul told the Colossians he was praying that they might arrive at the fullest knowledge of God's will through the spiritual gifts of wisdom and understanding. Therefore, they would be able to lead a life fully acceptable to You.[6] *(Read pp. 200-202 of "The Catholic Catechism" for information on the nature of the spiritual gifts of wisdom and understanding.)*

11. Lord, how important it is in our own age of confusion and uncertainty to know Your will; for instance, in moral matters. Thankfully, we have as our sure guide in this area, the Pope, the Successor of St. Peter and we also have the certain teaching of the bishops who teach in union with the Pope as their head. Please help us, Jesus, to accept their teaching with humility and love. *(An excellent presentation on the infallibility of the teaching role of the Pope and bishops is found on pp. 224-236 of "The Modern Catholic Catechism.")*

12. Most Sacred Heart of Jesus, may we also increase in our experiential knowledge of You through our close and constant contact with You in prayer. May this relationship inspire us to have an even greater desire to share You with others, so that they too may know You as their intimate Friend.

13. Finally, Jesus, St. Paul warns the Colossians not to exchange their freedom as

Christians for a merely rational philosophy.[7] Pure human reasoning, by itself, can never free us from sin and eternal death, no matter how true it may be. It can never free us to love You and others unselfishly, granting us true and lasting happiness. Only You can do that.

14. Therefore, Lord, help us not to lose the virtue of faith by which we accept You as our Savior and Lord, and by which we accept Your saving doctrine given by You to the Apostles, and through them to their successors, the bishops of Your Holy Catholic Church. It is the gift of faith that leads to the freedom which You alone can give; freedom from sin and freedom from everlasting death.

15. Most Sacred Heart of Jesus, may our faith in You never waver. You Who are the only Way to eternal life. Amen.

Try to read these Scripture passages and meditations several times a day in a reflective manner. Each time you do so, the Holy Spirit will give you more insights.

Please read and meditate on Chapter X, Paragraphs 1 to 8 of "Peaceful Seed Living," Volume II.

WEEK 1 DAY 2
Colossians 3:1-4:18

Life-giving union with the glorified Christ

3 ¹Since you have been brought back to true life with Christ, you must look for the things that are in heaven, where Christ is, ²sitting at God's right hand. ·Let your thoughts be on heavenly things, not on the ³things that are on the earth, ·because you have died, and now the life you have is hidden ⁴with Christ in God. ·But when Christ is revealed—and he is your life—you too will be revealed in all your glory with him. (C1)

III. EXHORTATION

General rules of Christian behavior

⁵ That is why you must kill everything in you that belongs only to earthly life: fornication, impurity, guilty passion, evil desires and especially greed, which is the same thing as ⁶worshiping a false god; ·all this is the sort of ⁷behavior that makes God angry. ·And it is the way in which you used to live when you were surrounded by people doing the same thing, ⁸but now you, of all people, must give all these things up: getting angry, being bad-tempered, spitefulness, abusive language and dirty talk; ⁹and never tell each other lies. You have stripped off your old behavior with your old ¹⁰self, ·and you have put on a new self which will progress toward true knowledge the more it is renewed in the image of its creator; ¹¹and in that image there is no room for distinction between Greek and Jew, between the circumcised or the uncircumcised, or between barbarian and Scythian, slave and free man. There is only Christ: he is everything and he is in everything. (C2) (C2) (C2) (C2) (C3) (C2) (C2) (C2) (C1) (C3) (C2) (C4) (C5)

¹² You are God's chosen race, his saints; he

loves you, and you should be clothed in sincere compassion, in kindness and humility, (C3)
13 gentleness and patience. •Bear with one another; forgive each other as soon as a quarrel (C3) begins. The Lord has forgiven you; now you
14 must do the same. •Over all these clothes, to keep them together and complete them, put
15 on love. •And may the peace of Christ reign (C3) in your hearts, because it is for this that you were called together as parts of one body. Always be thankful.
16 Let the message of Christ, in all its richness, find a home with you. Teach each other, (C1) and advise each other, in all wisdom. With (C3) gratitude in your hearts sing psalms and (C3)
17 hymns and inspired songs to God; •and never say or do anything except in the name of the Lord Jesus, giving thanks to God the Father (C3) through him.

The morals of the home and household

18 Wives, give way to your husbands, as you (C3)
19 should in the Lord. •Husbands, love your (C3)
20 wives and treat them with gentleness. •Children, be obedient to your parents always, be- (C3) cause that is what will please the Lord.
21 Parents, never drive your children to resent- (C2) ment or you will make them feel frustrated.

49

22 Slaves, be obedient to the men who are called your masters in this world; not only when you are under their eye, as if you had only to please men, but wholeheartedly, out (C3)
23 of respect for the Master. •Whatever your work is, put your heart into it as if it were for (C3)
24 the Lord and not for men, •knowing that the Lord will repay you by making you his heirs. It is Christ the Lord that you are serving; (C3)
25 anyone who does wrong will be repaid in (C2) kind and he does not favor one person more
1 than another. 4 Masters, make sure that your slaves are given what is just and fair, knowing (C3) that you too have a Master in heaven.

The apostolic spirit

2 Be persevering in your prayers and be (C3)
3 thankful as you stay awake to pray. •Pray for (C4) us especially, asking God to show us opportunities for announcing the message and pro- (C3) claiming the mystery of Christ, for the sake
4 of which I am in chains; •pray that I may proclaim it as clearly as I ought.
5 Be tactful with those who are not Chris- (C3) tians and be sure you make the best use of
6 your time with them. •Talk to them agreeably (C3) and with a flavor of wit, and try to fit your answers to the needs of each one.

Personal news

7 Tychicus will tell you all the news about me. He is a brother I love very much, and (C3) a loyal helper and companion in the service (C3)
8 of the Lord. •I am sending him to you precisely for this purpose: to give you news (C3)
9 about us and to reassure you. •With him I am sending Onesimus, that dear and faithful brother who is a fellow citizen of yours. They (C1) will tell you everything that is happening here.

Greetings and final wishes

10 Aristarchus, who is here in prison with me,

sends his greetings, and so does Mark, the cousin of Barnabas—you were sent some instructions about him; if he comes to you, give
11 him a warm welcome—·and Jesus Justus adds his greetings. Of all those who have come over from the Circumcision, these are the only ones actually working with me for the kingdom of God. They have been a great
12 comfort to me. ·Epaphras, your fellow citizen, sends his greetings; this servant of Christ Jesus never stops battling for you, praying that you will never lapse but always hold perfectly and securely to the will of
13 God. ·I can testify for him that he works hard for you, as well as for those at Laodicea and
14 Hierapolis. ·Greetings from my dear friend Luke, the doctor, and also from Demas.

15   Please give my greetings to the brothers at Laodicea and to Nympha and the church
16 which meets in her house. ·After this letter has been read among you, send it on to be read in the church of the Laodiceans; and get the letter from Laodicea for you to read
17 yourselves. ·Give Archippus this message, "Remember the service that the Lord wants you to do, and try to carry it out."
18   Here is a greeting in my own handwriting—PAUL. Remember the chains I wear. Grace be with you.

Week 1 Day 2
Four C's Reflections
on Colossians 3:1-4:18

1. Lord, in today's meditation, St. Paul states that we Christians have "been brought back to true life"[8] with You. He means, of course, that prior to our Baptism, we were spiritually dead. That is, we were cut off from the supernatural life of grace, which in Your unmatched charity, You merited for us by Your Cross and Passion. *(Read pp. 174-176 of "The Catholic Catechism" for a description of supernatural grace.)*

2. Before our Baptism, because we shared in the effects of the Fall, we did not have the life with God which leads to Heaven.* However, through Baptism, the sacrament of rebirth, we are spiritually reborn, being given a life of supernatural grace. Actually, because of this sacrament, we can now share in Your own divine life, which will remain with us for all eternity, providing we constantly strive on earth to remain Your friends. Even if we gravely sin, we can through Your infinite charity and mercy be restored to the supernatural or deiform life through Your sacrament of Penance.**

*(For information on the nature of the Fall, see "The Catholic Catechism." pp. 99-102. **See "The Catholic Catechism," for a penetrating presentation on the sacrament of Penance, pp. 481-500.)

3. Lord, how wonderful You are! You, Who love us so much that You freely suffered

and died for us so we might obtain life with You, which we in no way could have merited for ourselves! Thank You, Jesus! May we always express our thankfulness by leading lives pleasing to You!

4. Next, Lord, St. Paul reminds us that our thoughts must "be on heavenly things, not on things that are in the earth."[9]

5. By this he means we should place You first in our lives and to concentrate only on those things which will promote our supernatural or heavenly life with You in the here and now. When St. Paul says our thoughts should not be on things of earth, he does not mean only material things. He means anything on earth which leads us away from You and Your heavenly life and keeps us bound solely to life on this planet. Essentially, he had in mind things such as premarital or extramarital sex, masturbation, evil desires and greed.[10] *(For a summary of the Church's teaching on sexual pleasure read pp. 354-356 of "The Catholic Catechism.")*

6. Lord, grant us through Your grace to overcome all temptations to sin, so that we may continually live with You having our minds set on the things of Heaven. Jesus, Mary and Joseph! Pray for us!

7. Jesus, when St. Paul said we should have our thoughts set on heavenly things and not on things of earth he added, "because you have died, and now the life you have is hidden with Christ in God."[11] Obviously, here, he did not have reference to spiritual

death or to existence apart from the supernatural life of grace with You. What he meant was that when we were baptized we began to share mystically in Your death to sin.

8. In other words, through Baptism we are given the power to die to a "life" of sin which can only lead to hell. Through Your death and Resurrection, Lord, You in Your humanity overcame sin forever. You also conquered physical death, the penalty for sin, which, prior to Your victory on the Cross, pointed to eternal separation from Your divine presence in Heaven. *(For a fuller presentation on the theology of Baptism, see pp. 505-513 of "The Catholic Catechism.")*

9. Lord Jesus, may we die to sin every day and increasingly live for You wherein lies true happiness, peace and joy.

10. Our eyes, Lord, were also drawn in today's meditation to St. Paul's directive to forgive one another as soon as a quarrel begins.[12] This is really sound advice. It is expecially appropriate where quarrels occur frequently between husbands and wives, between children in a family, and between the children and their parents. If there is no forgiveness, divisions take place, contributing to family disunity and to separation and divorce. The only victor in such situations is the devil.

11. Lord, St. Paul gives us an incentive for forgiveness when he says we should forgive one another as You have forgiven us. How can we expect Your forgiveness and fail to forgive others? The "Our Father" makes this point crystal clear. "Forgive us our trespasses, as we forgive those who trespass against us." Elsewhere, St. Paul writes, "Even if you are angry, you must not sin: never let the sun set on your anger or else you will give the devil a foothold."[13] If couples would follow this advice by kissing and making up before going to sleep, a great many separations and divorces would be avoided.

12. Jesus, Mary and Joseph, we earnestly ask Your protection for our families. Instill into our hearts a willingness to forgive those who quarrel with us, or who offend us for whatever reason.

13. Lord, in today's Scripture reading, we discovered another piece of practical advice. This time it dealt with how to be Your

instruments in the conversion of non-Christians to Christianity. St. Paul says we should be tactful, making the best use of our time. We should also speak agreeably with a sense of humor. Moreover, we should tailor our answers to their questions about the Faith to fit their needs.[14] We imagine this advice would be suitable for non-practicing Christians as well.

14. Lord, inspire us constantly to seek the conversion of others to the Faith. May Your Holy Spirit also place into our minds the proper words to use in any given situation. Amen.

Try to read these Scripture passages and meditations in a reflective manner every day. The Holy Spirit will reveal more insights to you each time you do so.

Please read and meditate on Chapter X, Paragraphs 9 to 22 of "Peaceful Seed Living," Volume II.

WEEK 1 DAY 3
1 Thessalonians 1:1-2:20

1 Thessalonians

THE FIRST LETTER OF PAUL TO THE CHURCH IN THESSALONIKA

Address

1 From Paul, Silvanus and Timothy, to the Church in Thessalonika which is in God the Father and the Lord Jesus Christ; wishing you grace and peace.

Thanksgiving and congratulations

2 We always mention you in our prayers and
3 thank God for you all, ·and constantly remember before God our Father how you have shown your faith in action, worked for love and persevered through hope, in our Lord Jesus Christ.
4 We know, brothers, that God loves you
5 and that you have been chosen, ·because when we brought the Good News to you, it came to you not only as words, but as power and as the Holy Spirit and as utter conviction. And you observed the sort of life we lived when we were with you, which was for your
6 instruction, ·and you were led to become imitators of us, and of the Lord; and it was with the joy of the Holy Spirit that you took to the gospel, in spite of the great opposition
7 all round you. ·This has made you the great example to all believers in Macedonia and

8 Achaia •since it was from you that the word of the Lord started to spread—and not only throughout Macedonia and Achaia, for the news of your faith in God has spread everywhere. We do not need to tell other people 9 about it: •other people tell us how we started the work among you, how you broke with idolatry when you were converted to God and became servants of the real, living God; 10 and how you are now waiting for Jesus, his Son, whom he raised from the dead, to come from heaven to save us from the retribution which is coming.

Paul's example in Thessalonika

1 You know yourselves, my brothers, that our visit to you has not proved ineffectual.
2 We had, as you know, been given rough treatment and been grossly insulted at Philippi, and it was our God who gave us the courage to proclaim his Good News to you 3 in the face of great opposition. •We have not taken to preaching because we are deluded, 4 or immoral, or trying to deceive anyone; •it was God who decided that we were fit to be

entrusted with the Good News, and when we
are speaking, we are not trying to please men (C2)
but God, *who can read our inmost thoughts.*^a (C3)
5 You know very well, and we can swear it
before God, that never at any time have our
speeches been simply flattery, or a cover for (C2)
6 trying to get money; ·nor have we ever (C2)
looked for any special honor from men, ei- (C2)
7 ther from you or anybody else, ·when we
could have imposed ourselves on you with (C2)
full weight, as apostles of Christ.

Instead, we were unassuming. Like a (C3)
mother feeding and looking after her own
8 children, ·we felt so devoted and protective (C3)
toward you, and had come to love you so
much, that we were eager to hand over to you
not only the Good News but our whole lives
9 as well. ·Let me remind you, brothers, how (C3)
hard we used to work, slaving night and day (C4)
so as not to be a burden on any one of you
while we were proclaiming God's Good
10 News to you. ·You are witnesses, and so is (C3)
God, that our treatment of you, since you
became believers, has been impeccably right (C1)
11 and fair. ·You can remember how we treated
every one of you as a father treats his chil- (C3)
12 dren, ·teaching you what was right, encourag- (C3)
ing you and appealing to you to live a life
worthy of God, who is calling you to share (C3)
the glory of his kingdom.

The faith and the patience of the Thessalonians

13 Another reason why we constantly thank
God for you is that as soon as you heard the (C3)
message that we brought you as God's message, you accepted it for what it really is,
God's message and not some human thinking; and it is still a living power among you
14 who believe it. ·For you, my brothers, have (C1)
been like the churches of God in Christ Jesus
which are in Judaea, in suffering the same
treatment from your own countrymen as they (C2)

59

15 have suffered from the Jews, ·the people who (C2)
put the Lord Jesus to death, and the prophets (C2)
too. And now they have been persecuting us, (C2)
and acting in a way that cannot please God (C2)
and makes them the enemies of the whole
16 human race, ·because they are hindering us (C2)
from preaching to the pagans and trying to (C2)
save them. They never stop trying *to finish
off the sins they have begun,*[b] but retribution (C2)
is overtaking them at last.

Paul's anxiety

17   A short time after we had been separated
from you—in body but never in thought,
brothers—we had an especially strong desire
and longing to see you face to face again, (C3)
18 and we tried hard to come and visit you; I,
Paul, tried more than once, but Satan pre- (C4)
19 vented us. ·What do you think is our pride
and our joy? You are; and you will be *the
crown* of which we shall be *proudest* in the
presence of our Lord Jesus when he comes;
20 you are our pride and our joy.

60

Week 1 Day 3
Four C's Reflections
on 1 Thessalonians 1:1-2:20

1. Most Compassionate Lord, in reading St. Paul's First Letter to the Thessalonians one immediately discovers evidence of his immense love for the Christians at Thessolonika. It is apparent also that he was particularly pleased they had accepted the Gospel of salvation, in spite of much opposition. *(Be sure to read the introductory remarks about 1 and 2 Thessalonians beginning on p. 25 of this book.)*

2. Lord, in our day, we find our belief in You and in Your Gospel continually threatened by opposition both within and outside the Church. But it is the internal opposition that disturbs us the most. Not infrequently we run across articles written by "Catholics," who reject and question many aspects of Catholic doctrine.

3. Because of this internal opposition, many of us find ourselves confused especially about moral doctrine. And when this opposition is added to by those from outside the Church, it becomes even more difficult to remain faithful to Your unchangeable teaching, kept untarnished by the Popes since the time of Peter.

4. Jesus, Our Savior and invisible Head of the Church on earth, by the power of Your Holy Spirit help us always to accept as

necessary for salvation only that doctrine taught and approved by the Holy Roman Pontiff. As St. Peter's successor, he is Your chief spiritual representative on earth and has been given the gift of doctrinal infallibility to guide us into all truth. Therefore, help us to reject all teaching not upheld by the Roman Pontiff, even if it is proposed as true by hundreds of thousands of theologians. *(For information on papal infallibility see "The Catholic Catechism," pp. 223-224.)*

5. Lord, also in today's Scripture reading, St. Paul writes of the Thessalonians' conversion from the false gods of paganism to the Trinitarian God of Christianity.[15] However, conversion of the mind and will to God the Father, God the Son and God the Holy Spirit must be an on-going occurrence, as opposed to something which happens only once in a lifetime. *(For a presentation on the doctrine of the Trinity, see "The Catholic Catechism," pp. 63-67.)*

6. With the aid of Your grace, we must daily turn from sin and selfishness and dedicate ourselves anew to God. This can be accomplished by fervent prayer, especially within the context of the Mass, where we can unite ourselves to the Father through Your eternal sacrifice. Moreover, when we receive You at Holy Communion we are given graces to renew and refresh us spiritually. Therefore we are enabled to perform our daily tasks in a Christian manner. *(Read pp. 465-468 of "The Catholic Catechism" for a discussion of the Mass as a sacrificial action, and read pp. 471-479 with respect to Holy Communion.)*

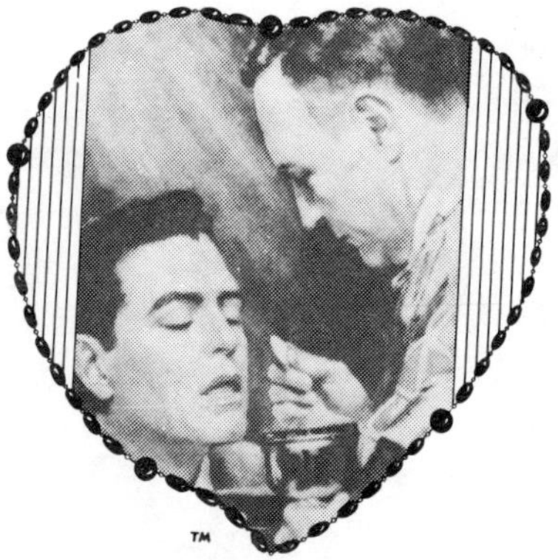

7. Inspire us daily, Lord, to turn from our wickedness and live in Your abiding presence. And may Your presence be so evident in our own lives that many others will be encouraged to turn to You and remain with You as Your friend.

8. Most Sacred Heart of Jesus, in our meditation for today, St. Paul compares himself to a "mother, feeding and looking after her own children..."[16] These words reminded us of Your expression of concern for Your fellow Jews at Jerusalem. "Jerusalem, Jerusalem, you that kill the prophets and stone those that are sent to you! How often I have longed to gather your children, as a hen gathers her chicks under her wings, and you refused!"[17]

9. St. Paul also used the image of a father in addressing the Thessalonians.

10. "You can remember how we treated every one of you as a father treats his children, teaching you what was right, encouraging you and appealing to you to live a life worthy of God, who is calling you to share the glory of his kingdom."[18]

11. These passages remind us, Lord, that Catholic parents have an obligation to meet their children's supernatural needs. They must do their best to provide them with the teaching of the Church, and with the graces received through the sacraments and prayer. Lord, how important it is to nourish and foster the spiritual life of children. Please always impress upon parents that this is primarily their task, and not that of others who may assist them. And may they never tire of turning to You in prayer and in the sacraments, so they can become increasingly holy and set shining examples for their children to follow.

12. Jesus, we noted in an earlier meditation that St. Paul contrasted the message of the Gospel with mere human learning.[19] He also does this in the present meditation,[20] when he tells us the Gospel is God's message. That is, it comes from God the Father through You. It is divine revelation, not simply the product of human reasoning. It is not just another philosophy about the nature, origin and purpose of man and the universe. No, Lord, in Your Gospel You have revealed Yourself and Your will for us. In it, whether in Scripture or Tradition, we have all we need to know for our salvation. Thankfully, You have also given us that supernatural gift of faith whereby we can believe what You have revealed. Anything that is contrary to Your revelation is erroneous and must be rejected. This holds true even if one hundred billion of our fellow humans thought to the contrary.
(See "The Catholic Catechism," pp. 41-42. Here Scripture and Tradition are distinguished.)

13. Lord, grant us such faith in Your authentic doctrine, received and interpreted by Your Catholic Church, that we will never fall away from the words of eternal life. Amen.

Try to read these Scripture passages and meditations in a reflective manner every day. The Holy Spirit will reveal more insights to you each time you do so.

Please read and meditate on Chapter X, Paragraphs 23 to 31 of "Peaceful Seed Living," Volume II.

WEEK 1 DAY 4
I Thessalonians 3:1-5:28

Timothy's mission to Thessalonika

3 ¹When we could not bear the waiting any longer, we decided it would be best to be ²left without a companion at Athens, and •sent our brother Timothy, who is God's helper in (C3) spreading the Good News of Christ, to keep ³you firm and strong in the faith •and prevent (C4) any of you from being unsettled by the present troubles. As you know, these are bound ⁴to come our way: •when we were with you, we warned you that we must expect to have persecutions to bear, and that is what has (C2) ⁵happened now, as you have found out. •That is why, when I could not stand waiting any longer, I sent to assure myself of your faith: (C1) I was afraid the Tempter*a* might have tried you too hard, and all our work might have (C2) been wasted.

**Paul thanks God for good reports
of the Thessalonians**

6 However, Timothy is now back from you and he has given us good news of your faith (C1) and your love, telling us that you always (C3) remember us with pleasure and want to see 7 us quite as much as we want to see you. •And (C3) so, brothers, your faith has been a great com- (C1) fort to us in the middle of our own troubles 8 and sorrows; •now we can breathe again, as 9 you are still holding firm in the Lord. •How (C4) can we thank God enough for you, for all the joy we feel before our God on your account? (C3) 10 We are earnestly praying night and day to be (C3, able to see you face to face again and make up any shortcomings in your faith.

11 May God our Father himself, and our Lord Jesus Christ, make it easy for us to 12 come to you. •May the Lord be generous in increasing your love and make you love one (C3) another and the whole human race as much 13 as we love you. •And may he so confirm your hearts in holiness that you may be blameless (C2) in the sight of our God and Father when our Lord Jesus Christ comes *with all his saints.*

Live in holiness and charity

4 ¹ Finally, brothers, we urge you and appeal to you in the Lord Jesus to make more and more progress in the kind of life that you are meant to live: the life that God wants, as you learned from us, and as you are already living ² it. ·You have not forgotten the instructions we gave you on the authority of the Lord Jesus.

³ What God wants is for you all to be holy. He wants you to keep away from fornication, ⁴ and each one of you to know how to use the body that belongs to him*a* in a way that is holy ⁵ and honorable, ·not giving way to selfish lust ⁶ like *the pagans who do not know God.b* ·He wants nobody at all ever to sin by taking advantage of a brother in these matters; the Lord always punishes sins of that sort, as we ⁷ told you before and assured you. ·We have been called by God to be holy, not to be ⁸ immoral; ·in other words, anyone who objects is not objecting to a human authority, but to God, *who gives you his* Holy *Spirit.c*

⁹ As for loving our brothers, there is no need for anyone to write to you about that, since you have learned from God yourselves ¹⁰ to love one another, ·and in fact this is what you are doing with all the brothers throughout the whole of Macedonia. However, we do urge you, brothers, to go on making even ¹¹ greater progress ·and to make a point of living quietly, attending to your own business and earning your living, just as we told you ¹² to, ·so that you are seen to be respectable by those outside the Church, though you do not have to depend on them.

The dead and the living at the time of the Lord's coming

¹³ We want you to be quite certain, brothers, about those who have died,*d* to make sure

that you do not grieve about them, like the
14 other people who have no hope. ·We believe
that Jesus died and rose again, and that it will
be the same for those who have died in Jesus:
15 God will bring them with him. ·We can tell
you this from the Lord's own teaching, that
any of us who are left alive until the Lord's
coming will not have any advantage over
16 those who have died. ·At the trumpet of God,
the voice of the archangel will call out the
command and the Lord himself will come
down from heaven; those who have died in
17 Christ will be the first to rise, ·and then those
of us who are still alive will be taken up in
the clouds, together with them, to meet the
Lord in the air. So we shall stay with the Lord
18 for ever. ·With such thoughts as these you
should comfort one another.

Watchfulness while awaiting the coming of the Lord

1 **5** You will not be expecting us to write anything to you, brothers, about "times and
2 seasons," ·since you know very well that the
Day of the Lord is going to come like a thief
3 in the night. ·It is when people are saying,
"How quiet and peaceful it is," that the worst
suddenly happens, as suddenly as labor pains
come on a pregnant woman; and there will
be no way for anybody to evade it.

4 But it is not as if you live in the dark, my
brothers, for that Day to overtake you like a
5 thief. ·No, you are all sons of light and sons
of the day: we do not belong to the night or
6 to darkness, ·so we should not go on sleep-
ing, as everyone else does, but stay wide
7 awake and sober. ·Night is the time for sleep-
8 ers to sleep and drunkards to be drunk, ·but
we belong to the day and we should be sober;
let us put on faith and love for a *breastplate,*
9 and the hope of *salvation* for a *helmet.* ·God
never meant us to experience the Retribution, but to win salvation through our Lord

10 Jesus Christ, ·who died for us so that, alive
or dead, we should still live united to him. (C3)
11 So give encouragement to each other, and (C3)
keep strengthening one another, as you do (C4)
already.

Some demands made by life in community

12 We appeal to you, my brothers, to be considerate to those who are working amongst (C3)
you and are above you in the Lord as your
13 teachers. ·Have the greatest respect and af- (C3)
fection for them because of their work.
14 Be at peace among yourselves. ·And this (C3)
is what we ask you to do, brothers: warn the (C3)
idlers, give courage to those who are appre- (C2)
hensive, care for the weak and be patient with (C3)

15 everyone. ·Make sure that people do not try
to take revenge; you must all think of what (C2)
is best for each other and for the community. (C3)
16-18 Be happy at all times; ·pray constantly; ·and (C3)
for all things give thanks to God, because this (C4)
is what God expects you to do in Christ (C3)
Jesus.
19 20 Never try to suppress the Spirit ·or treat (C2)
21 the gift of prophecy with contempt; ·think (C2)
before you do anything—hold on to what is (C4)
22 good ·and *avoid every* form of *evil*. (C2)

Closing prayer and farewell

23 May the God of peace make you perfect
and holy; and may you all be kept safe and (C3)
blameless, spirit, soul and body, for the com- (C2)

24 ing of our Lord Jesus Christ. ·God has called
you and he will not fail you.
25 Pray for us, my brothers. (C3)
26 Greet all the brothers with the holy kiss. (C3)
27 My orders, in the Lord's name, are that this
letter is to be read to all the brothers.
28 The grace of our Lord Jesus Christ be with (C3)
you.

Week 1 Day 4
Four C's Reflections
on I Thessalonians 3:1-5:28

1. Dearest Lord Jesus, in today's Scripture lesson St. Paul warned the Thessalonians that Christians can expect trouble in their lives, including persecutions.[21] This reminds us of Your own words to Your Apostles when You said:

2. "They will expell you from the synagogues, and indeed the hour is coming when anyone who kills you will think he is doing a holy duty for God. They will do these things because they have never known either the Father or myself."[22]

3. Furthermore, You declared:

4. "Happy are you when people abuse you and persecute you and speak all kinds of calumny against you on my account. Rejoice

and be glad, for your reward will be great in heaven."[23]

5. In the Acts of the Apostles we see these words fulfilled when the Apostles were whipped for refusing to comply with an order from the Jewish leaders to stop evangelizing. "And so they left the presence of the Sanhedrin glad to have the honor of suffering humiliation for the sake of the name (of Jesus)."[24] *(The Sanhedrin was the governing council of the Jews.)*

6. Lord, in our own day, we also can expect to suffer in one way or another at the hands of others, if we are among your faithful followers. There are the obvious examples of persecution which Christians face today in countries such as the Soviet Union. There, Christians can be put to death, imprisoned, tortured, and refused decent jobs. But Your loyal followers can also be persecuted in a society such as our own.

7. A physician or a nurse, for instance, can be expelled from some hospital staffs for refusing to perform or assist in an abortion. Teachers can be denied jobs because they hold Christian principles which sharply contrast with the values and principles of school administrators and of many of their colleagues in the teaching profession. Children can be ostracised for refusing to enter into activities which Scripture and the Church forbid. Promotions can be denied to individuals who refuse to participate in unjust practices. And You Yourself warned that

Your true disciples would even be persecuted by members of their own families. "A man's enemies will be those of his own household."[25]

8. Jesus, when in fact we are faced with persecutions, we who are so weak, are often greatly tempted to deny You in order to avoid suffering. Please strengthen us with Your grace and inspire us not to yield to such temptations, reminding us of Your promise of eternal rewards for those who remain in Your friendship.[26]

9. Lord, in today's meditation, St. Paul made it very clear that the ability to love one another sacrificially comes from You. "May the Lord be generous in increasing your love and make you love one another and the whole human race as much as we love you."[27] Since this is the case, we must never tire of asking You for an increase of the supernatural grace of seed-charity.

10. We should realize, however, that genuine Christian charity for others is not to be confused with always doing what others might ask of us. No, we must love them only as You have loved us. That is, not only sacrificially, but also according to the principles of Christian morality. Thus, it would not be truly charitable to commit adultery or to perform homosexual acts with those who may desire them. Nor would it be truly charitable to spoil others, or to lie, steal and cheat for them. And sometimes, our love

for others must be in the form of denials, since that is what would be best for them. At other times, our Christian love for others might take the form of discipline, since this too might be what is best for them, as in the case of parents disciplining their children.

11. Dearest Savior, St. Paul urges the Thessalonians to make progress in leading a Christian life.[28] Applying this to ourselves, we should not be satisfied with maintaining the status-quo with respect to our spiritual state. We should become each day a little more holy, a little more like Yourself, a little more like Your Blessed Mother and St. Joseph, and a little more like all the saints.

12. We, who are so accustomed to the idea of progress in secular things, should not find it difficult to apply the same idea to the spiritual plane. On the other hand, we should not be surprised to experience momentary setbacks due to our inherent tendency to sin. Nonetheless, with constancy, we will notice that our

pet sins usually become less frequent, and in some instances may disappear altogether. *(For more on our inherent, unreasonable tendency to sin, i.e., concupisence, see "The Catholic Catechism," pp. 426-427, 507.)*

13. Lord, grant that we may never stop struggling against sin. May we persevere and make daily progress in leading a life of holiness. We know that in doing so we will be rewarded in eternity according to our efforts and in terms of varying degrees of peace and happiness. And in this world we will be better able to help others become more holy. This is so because as we become increasingly like You, we become more effective instruments for Your work of salvation and sanctification.

14. Jesus, St. Paul encouraged the Thessalonians to be considerate of those who taught them Christian (Catholic) doctrine. Then he added, "Have the greatest respect and affection for them because of their work."[29] This certainly makes sense, Lord, since they, as Your representatives, have been entrusted with the teaching which leads to eternal life. We, of course, should respect all who teach what is true and good, but the teachers of authentic Catholic doctrine should be especially esteemed, because of the vital nature of their work.

15. Consequently, we should respect above all the Pope, who is the chief teacher of Christians, and we should respect also the bishops who teach in union with him. But, we should highly regard as well priests, deacons,

nuns, lay teachers and parents who teach the Catholic Faith.

16. Lord, we very much need teachers today who are loyal to the doctrine of the Church of Rome. We humbly ask You to inspire many to dedicate their lives for this purpose so increasing numbers of people may receive the words of eternal life. And may parents faithfully and regularly teach the Catholic Faith to their children, not only with their words but also by their actions. Amen.

Try to read these Scripture passages and meaitations in a reflective manner every day. The Holy Spirit will reveal more insights to you each time you do so.

Please read and meditate on Chapter X, Paragraphs 32 to 44 of "Peaceful Seed Living," Volume II.

WEEK 1 DAY 5
2 Thessalonians 1:1-3:18

2 Thessalonians

THE SECOND LETTER OF PAUL TO THE CHURCH IN THESSALONIKA

Address

1 From Paul, Silvanus and Timothy, to the Church in Thessalonika which is in God our Father and the Lord Jesus Christ; ·wishing you grace and peace from God the Father (C3) and the Lord Jesus Christ.

Thanksgiving and encouragement.
The Last Judgment

3 We feel we must be continually thanking (C3) God for you, brothers; quite rightly, because your faith is growing so wonderfully and the (C1) love that you have for one another never (C4)

4 stops increasing; •and among the churches of
God we can take special pride in you for your
constancy and faith under all the persecu-
5 tions and troubles you have to bear. •It all

shows that God's judgment is just, and the
purpose of it is that you may be found worthy
of the kingdom of God; it is for the sake of
this that you are suffering now.

6 God will very rightly repay with injury
7 those who are injuring you, •and reward you,
who are suffering now, with the same peace
as he will give us, when the Lord Jesus appears from heaven with the angels of his
8 power. •He will come *in flaming fire* to im-
pose the penalty on *all who do not acknowledge God*[a] and *refuse to accept* the Good
9 News of our Lord Jesus. •It will be their
punishment to be lost eternally, excluded
from the presence of the Lord and from the
10 *glory of his strength* •*on that day* when he
comes *to be glorified among his saints* and
seen in his glory[b] by all who believe in him;
and you are believers, through our witness.
11 Knowing this, we pray continually that our
God will make you worthy of his call, and by
his power fulfill all your desires for goodness
and complete all that you have been doing
12 through faith; •because in this way *the name*
of our Lord Jesus Christ *will be glorified* in
you and you in him, by the grace of our God
and the Lord Jesus Christ.

The coming of the Lord and the prelude to it

1 2 To turn now, brothers, to the coming of
our Lord Jesus Christ and how we shall
2 all be gathered round him: •please do not get
excited too soon or alarmed by any predic-
tion or rumor or any letter claiming to come
from us, implying that the Day of the Lord
3 has already arrived. •Never let anyone deceive you in this way.

It cannot happen until the Great Revolt has

taken place and the Rebel, the Lost One, has
4 appeared. •This is the Enemy, the one who
 claims to be so much *greater than all* that
 men call "god," so much greater than anything that is worshiped, that *he enthrones
 himself* in *God's* sanctuary and claims that
5 he is God. •Surely you remember me telling
6 you about this when I was with you? •And
 you know, too, what is still holding him back
 from appearing before his appointed time.
7 Rebellion is at its work already, but in secret, and the one who is holding it back has
8 first to be removed •before the Rebel appears
 openly. The Lord *will kill him with the breath
 of his mouth*[a] and will annihilate him with his
 glorious appearance at his coming.
9 But when the Rebel comes, Satan will set
 to work: there will be all kinds of miracles
 and a deceptive show of signs and portents,
10 and everything evil that can deceive those
 who are bound for destruction because they
 would not grasp the love of the truth which
11 could have saved them. •The reason why
 God is sending a power to delude them and
12 make them believe what is untrue •is to condemn all who refused to believe in the truth
 and chose wickedness instead.

Encouragement to persevere

13 But we feel that we must be continually
 thanking God for you, brothers whom the
 Lord loves, because God chose you from the
 beginning to be saved by the sanctifying
14 Spirit and by faith in the truth. •Through the
 Good News that we brought he called you
 to this so that you should share the glory of
15 our Lord Jesus Christ. •Stand firm, then,
 brothers, and keep the traditions that we
 taught you, whether by word of mouth or by
16 letter. •May our Lord Jesus Christ himself,
 and God our Father who has given us his love
 and, through his grace, such inexhaustible

79

17 comfort and such sure hope, •comfort you (C3)
and strengthen you in everything good that
you do or say.

1 **3** Finally, brothers, pray for us; pray that the (C3)
Lord's message may spread quickly, and
be received with honour as it was among you;
2 and pray that we may be preserved from the (C3)
interference of bigoted and evil people, for
3 faith is not given to everyone. •But the Lord (C1)
is faithful, and he will give you strength and
4 guard you from the evil one, •and we, in the
Lord, have every confidence that you are do- (C1)
ing and will go on doing all that we tell you.
5 May the Lord turn your hearts toward the
love of God and the fortitude of Christ. (C3)

Against idleness and disunity

6 In the name of the Lord Jesus Christ, we
urge you, brothers, to keep away from any
of the brothers who refuses to work or to live (C2)
according to the tradition we passed on to
you.
7 You know how you are supposed to imitate (C3)
us: now we were not idle when we were with (C2)
8 you, •nor did we ever have our meals at anyone's table without paying for them; no, we
worked night and day, slaving and straining, (C4)

9 so as not to be a burden on any of you. ·This was not because we had no right to be, but in order to make ourselves an example for you to follow.
10 We gave you a rule when we were with you: not to let anyone have any food if he
11 refused to do any work. ·Now we hear that there are some of you who are living in idleness, doing no work themselves but interfer-
12 ing with everyone else's. ·In the Lord Jesus Christ, we order and call on people of this kind to go on quietly working and earning the food that they eat.
13 My brothers, never grow tired of doing
14 what is right. ·If anyone refuses to obey what I have written in this letter, take note of him and have nothing to do with him, so that he
15 will feel that he is in the wrong; ·though you are not to regard him as an enemy but as a brother in need of correction.

Prayer and farewell wishes

16 May the Lord of peace himself give you peace all the time and in every way. The Lord be with you all.
17 From me, PAUL, these greetings in my own handwriting, which is the mark of genuineness in every letter; this is my own writing.
18 May the grace of our Lord Jesus Christ be with you all.

Week 1 Day 5
Four C's Reflections
on 2 Thessalonians 1:1-3:18

1. Most Sacred Heart of Jesus, in First Thessalonians, St. Paul urged the Christians in Thessalonika to make progress in sanctity, and in Second Thessalonians, he notes they have, in fact, advanced in holiness. He particularly draws attention to their increases in faith and charity.[30]

2. We see suggested here a parallel with natural growth. If a youngster eats and sleeps properly and takes good care of his body, he will continue to grow to maturity. And in the life of grace, if one continues to pray fervently and make proper use of all the graces available to him, he will continue to grow spiritually and eventually reach a supernatural maturity, which is the state of sanctity. However, just as disease tends to hinder our natural growth and development, sin hinders our supernatural development. So it should be no surprise that the widely accepted materialistic and pleasure-oriented values of our times have had a devastating effect on spiritual growth.

3. Lord, may we continue to grow daily in our spiritual lives so we may become a saintly people dedicated to You and to Your will. To help us achieve this goal, inspire us to continuously desire sanctity and to despise sin and always resist sinful temptations.

4. Jesus, St. Paul implies that the persecu-

tions and sufferings the Thessalonians endured as Your followers were a means of divine testing. "The purpose of it is that you may be found worthy of the kingdom of God; it is for the sake of this that you are suffering now."[31] St. Peter says something similar.

5. "This is a cause of great joy for you, even though you may for a short time have to bear being plagued by all sorts of trials; so that, when Jesus Christ is revealed (at the end of time), your faith will have been tested and proved like gold — only it is more precious than gold, which is corruptible even though it bears testing by fire — and then you will have praise and glory and honor."[32]

6. In other words, Jesus, one of the chief reasons You permit evil is because by resisting it with the aid of Your grace we become more holy. Consequently, we become more worthy of Your heavenly Kingdom. Very likely, if we were to be granted entrance into Your Kingdom without any effort on our part, most of us would not even begin to appreciate the sacrifices You have made for us. But by imitating You in making sacrifices and through suffering, we gradually learn how much love You have for us.

7. Jesus, the key to surviving the trials of life is to persevere in our love for You and for others for Your sake. You Yourself said, "You will be hated by all men on account of my name; but the man who stands firm to the end will be saved."[33]

8. Most Merciful and Most Loving Lord,

help us to persevere in Your friendship to the very end by the exercise of charitable thoughts, words and deeds so we may eventually see You face to face, and eternally enjoy the companionship of Your angels and saints.

9. Lord, St. Paul told the Christians at Thessalonika God had chosen them from the very beginning "to be saved by the sanctifying Spirit and by faith in the truth."[34] We see here then the great love God the Father has for those whom He foresaw from all eternity would accept Him freely by the gift of faith. These also would have had access to the gift of constancy in order to persevere in the way of sanctity until their deaths and be saved eternally.[35] But man's eternal salvation, Lord, would not have been possible at all without Your first meriting it for him on the Cross of Calvary. Our salvation comes first of all as Your free gift. It is only then, through the daily exercise of faith and charity, that we can keep it and deepen our friendship with You Who love us so much. *(Read pp. 80-81 of*

"The Catholic Catechism" for a discussion of God's foreknowledge and human freedom. See also *"Predestination"* on p. 434 of the *"Modern Catholic Dictionary."*

10. Lord Jesus, St. Paul also stresses the importance of work for Christians. More than once in his writings, he says how hard he worked so he would not be a burden on his fellow Christians, and also that they might have an example to follow. Yet there were some in Thessalonika who refused to work, thus burdening the whole community of believers. In response to this lack of charity, St. Paul ruled such persons were to be denied food and to be shunned.[36]

11. Most Sacred Heart of Jesus, as You well know, we live in a time in which work is generally not held as a virtue. Rather, there is a tendency to see it as an evil to be avoided as much as possible. Yet, from the very beginning God commanded that we must work.[37]

12. Dear Lord, if we are not willing to work for a living, we are not likely to put forth the constant effort needed to retain Your gift of salvation. Nor are we likely to work for the salvation of others.

13. Lord, continually inspire in us a desire to work, thereby avoiding the evil of sloth (laziness) which the Church teaches is one of the seven deadly sins. Moreover, help those who want work to find it. *(For information on these sins read p. 81 of "The Modern Catholic Dictionary" under the heading, 'Capital Sins.')*

14. Jesus, when St. Paul told the Thessalonians to avoid those who would refuse to obey him, he was in fact exercising a rather strict form of charity. But he wanted to help the lazy people to realize they were in the wrong so they might repent and be reconciled to You and their fellow Christians. (38)

15. Lord, help parents to discipline their children whenever they need it. At the same time may they always do it with seed-charity, and may their children always realize they are loved, whether they are treated gently or severely. Amen.

Try to read these Scripture passages and meditations in a reflective manner every day. The Holy Spirit will reveal more insights to you each time you do so.

Please read and meditate on Chapter X, Paragraphs 45 to 54 of "Peaceful Seed Living," Volume II.

WEEK 1 DAY 6
I Timothy 1:1-2:15

1 Timothy

THE FIRST LETTER FROM PAUL TO TIMOTHY

Address

1 From Paul, apostle of Christ Jesus appointed by the command of God our sav-
2 ior and of Christ Jesus our hope, ·to Timothy, true child of mine in the faith; wishing you grace, mercy and peace from God the Father (C3) and from Christ Jesus our Lord.

Suppress the false teachers

3 As I asked you when I was leaving for Macedonia, please stay at Ephesus, to insist that certain people stop teaching strange doc- (C2)
4 trines ·and taking notice of myths and endless (C2) genealogies; these things are only likely to raise irrelevant doubts instead of furthering (C2) the designs of God which are revealed in
5 faith. ·The only purpose of this instruction is (C1) that there should be love, coming out of a (C3) pure heart, a clear conscience and a sincere (C2)
6 faith. ·There are some people who have gone (C1) off the straight course and taken a road that (C2)
7 leads to empty speculation; ·they claim to be doctors of the Law but they understand neither the arguments they are using nor the opinions they are upholding.

87

The purpose of the Law

8 We know, of course, that the Law is good, but only provided it is treated like any law,
9 in the understanding that laws are not framed for people who are good. On the contrary, they are for criminals and revolutionaries, for the irreligious and the wicked, for the sacrilegious and the irreverent; they are for people who kill their fathers or mothers and for
10 murderers, ·for those who are immoral with women or with boys or with men, for liars and for perjurers—and for everything else
11 that is contrary to the sound teaching ·that goes with the Good News of the glory of the blessed God, the gospel that was entrusted to me.

Paul on his own calling

12 I think Christ Jesus our Lord, who has given me strength, and who judged me faith-
13 ful enough to call me into his service ·even though I used to be a blasphemer and did all I could to injure and discredit the faith. Mercy, however, was shown me, because until I became a believer I had been acting in

14 ignorance; ·and the grace of our Lord filled me with faith and with the love that is in (C1)
15 Christ Jesus. ·Here is a saying that you can (C2) rely on and nobody should doubt: that Christ Jesus came into the world to save sinners. I
16 myself am the greatest of them; ·and if mercy (C2) has been shown to me, it is because Jesus Christ meant to make me the greatest evidence of his inexhaustible patience for all the other people who would later have to (C1)
17 trust in him to come to eternal life. ·To the eternal King, the undying, invisible and only God, be honor and glory for ever and ever. Amen.

Timothy's responsibility

18 Timothy, my son, these are the instructions that I am giving you: I ask you to remember the words once spoken over you by the prophets, and taking them to heart to
19 fight like a good soldier ·with faith and a good (C4) conscience for your weapons. Some people (C1) (C2) have put conscience aside and wrecked their
20 faith in consequence. ·I mean men like (C1) Hymenaeus and Alexander, whom I have handed over to Satan to teach them not to be (C3) blasphemous. (C2)

Liturgical prayer

2 1 My advice is that, first of all, there should be prayers offered for everyone—petitions, (C3)
2 intercessions and thanksgiving—·and especially for kings and others in authority, so that we may be able to live religious and
3 reverent lives in peace and quiet. ·To do this (C3)
4 is right, and will please God our savior: ·he wants everyone to be saved and reach full (C3)
5 knowledge of the truth. ·For there is only one (C1) God, and there is only one mediator between God and mankind, himself a man, Christ
6 Jesus, ·who sacrificed himself as a ransom for them all. He is the evidence of this, sent at

7 the appointed time, and •I have been named a herald and apostle of it and—I am telling the truth and no lie—a teacher of the faith and the truth to the pagans.

8 In every place, then, I want the men to lift their hands up reverently in prayer, with no anger or argument.

Women in the assembly

9 Similarly, I direct that women are to wear suitable clothes and to be dressed quietly and modestly, without braided hair or gold and jewelry or expensive clothes; their adorn-
10 ment is •to do the sort of good works that are proper for women who profess to be reli-
11 gious. •During instruction, a woman should
12 be quiet and respectful. •I am not giving permission for a woman to teach or to tell a man what to do. A woman ought not to speak,
13 because Adam was formed first and Eve aft-
14 erwards, •and it was not Adam who was led astray but the woman who was led astray and
15 fell into sin. •Nevertheless, she will be saved by childbearing, provided she lives a modest life and is constant in faith and love and holiness.

Week 1 Day 6
Four C's Reflections
on I Timothy 1:1-2:15

1. Most Holy Savior, in his First Letter to Timothy, St. Paul again emphasizes the importance of teaching only the doctrine which comes from God. Actually, he puts it in a more negative way by insisting that Timothy prohibit the teaching of strange doctrines, that is, doctrines which are alien to the true Faith.[39] *(Be sure to read the introductory remarks about I Timothy on p.26 of this book.)*

2. Today we are surrounded by a multitude of strange doctrines, which, in one way or another, undermine the Faith You taught St. Peter and the other Apostles. Therefore, to banish and oppose such ideas in a charitable manner is a great service to the Church.

3. The Pope and bishops are primarily responsible for rooting out all erroneous doctrine from the Church. But priests, deacons, Religious, lay teachers and parents also share this responsibility. Parents, for example, must make sure their children are taught only the true Faith, whether at home or elsewhere. If there is any doubt as to what the true Faith is, one can consult works such as Father Hardon's "The Catholic Catechism" and his "The Question and Answer Catholic Catechism."

4. We know also, Lord, the doctrine You entrusted to St. Peter and the other Apostles, is true and essentially unchangeable. Consequently, any teaching which basically contradicts the unchangeable teaching of the Church of Rome, the Church of Peter, is erroneous and must be rejected.

5. This is not to say that Your Catholic doctrine cannot grow and develop as the trunk and branches of a tree grow and develop from the roots. Thus, there can be clearer insights into Your teaching as time progresses. And there can be a variety of ways to express it. Nonetheless, this true growth and development never contradict what You and Your Apostles taught. Therefore, Catholic doctrine in its developed state, for instance, could never deny Your divinity, or Your Resurrection, or the indissolubility of marriage. Nor could it teach that sexual deviations were no longer sins.

6. Lord Jesus, through the power of Your Holy Spirit, help us to believe and teach regarding our salvation only what is taught by the Church of Rome. And help us to realize that by doing so, we are indeed performing a service of seed-charity.

7. Most Sacred Heart of Jesus, we noted with interest in today's reading, St. Paul's personal testimony to his unworthiness to be Your disciple.

8. "I thank Christ Jesus our Lord, who has given me strength, and who judged me faithful enough to call me into his service even though I used to be a blasphemer and did all I could to injure and discredit the faith. Mercy, however, was shown me, because until I became a believer I had been acting in ignorance; and the grace of our Lord filled me with faith and with the love that is in Christ Jesus... and if mercy has been shown to me, it is because Jesus Christ meant to make me

the greatest evidence of his inexhaustible patience for all the other people who would later have to trust in him to come to eternal life."[40]

9. This passage gives us so much hope, Lord. Few in the history of Your Church have been as holy as St. Paul. At the same time, there are few who persecuted the Church with the same or greater fervor.[41]

10. From all eternity, You knew the great potential the sinner Saul had for sanctity. Thus, at the proper moment, You inspired his conversion so he might serve You and Your Church in a manner few have equalled and, at the same time, gain his own eternal salvation.

11. St. Paul's example teaches us, Lord, that You did not die for us to make salvation possible because we were holy. Rather, sinners though we were, and still are, You have always seen our potential for sanctity. From eternity You knew many of us would respond positively to Your sacrificial love and persevere to the end in faith, hope and seed-charity so we could enjoy life with You forever.

12. St. Paul says You made him an example of Your inexhaustible patience towards us fallen human beings.[42] Because of Your saving action through him, we are given hope that we cannot only be saved from sin and eternal death, but actually acquire great sanctity as well.

13. Jesus, be patient with us unworthy sinners. When we fall, inspire us to repent and love You and others with greater intensity than before. And may the prayers of Your Blessed Mother, St. Joseph and all the saints confirm us in the path of sanctity.

14. Lord, we have noted in St. Paul's letters his continuous stress on prayer, and his First Letter to Timothy is no exception. But here he also encourages prayers for non-Christian rulers so that Your Church might exist free from persecution. [43]

15. St. Paul, if he were on earth today, would urge more of the same since there are millions of Christians in various parts of the world who are openly persecuted by non-Christian authorities.

16. We, who are relatively free from this kind of torment should pray for the courage and perseverance of our persecuted fellow Christians. We should also pray for their rulers so they will be converted or at least treat their Christian subjects with justice and allow them freedom of worship.

17. Lord, we offer up these petitions here and now. Moreover, in accordance with Our Lady's instructions at Fatima, we pray for the conversion of Russia. Amen.

Try to read these Scripture passages and meditations in a reflective manner every day. The Holy Spirit will reveal more insights to you each time you do so.

Please read and meditate on Chapter X, Paragraphs 55 to 71 of "Peaceful Seed Living," Volume II.

WEEK 1 DAY 7
1 Timothy 3:1-4:16

The elder-in-charge

3 ¹Here is a saying that you can rely on: To want to be a presiding elder*ᵃ* is to want to ²do a noble work. •That is why the president must have an impeccable character. He must (C2) not have been married more than once, and he must be temperate, discreet and courte- (C3) ³ous, hospitable and a good teacher; •not a (C3) heavy drinker, nor hot-tempered, but kind (C2) and peaceable. He must not be a lover of (C3) ⁴money. •He must be a man who manages his (C2) own family well and brings his children up (C3) ⁵to obey him and be well-behaved: •how can any man who does not understand how to manage his own family have responsibility (C2) ⁶for the church of God? •He should not be a new convert, in case pride might turn his head and then he might be condemned as ⁷the devil was condemned. •It is also necessary that people outside the Church should speak well of him, so that he never gets a bad reputation and falls into the devil's (C2) trap.

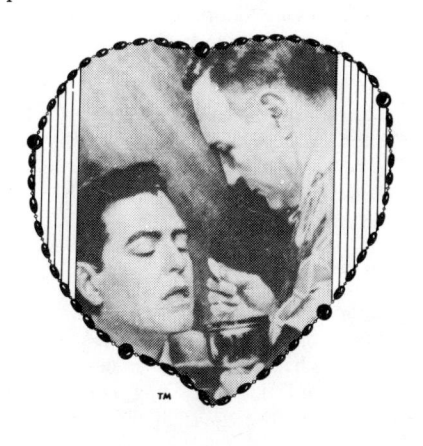

Deacons

8 In the same way, deacons must be respectable men whose word can be trusted, moderate in the amount of wine they drink and with 9 no squalid greed for money. ·They must be (C2) conscientious believers in the mystery of the (C1) 10 faith. ·They are to be examined first, and only (C2) admitted to serve as deacons if there is nothing 11 against them. ·In the same way, the women must be respectable, not gossips but 12 sober and quite reliable. ·Deacons must not (C3) have been married more than once, and must be men who manage their children and fami- (C3) 13 lies well. ·Those of them who carry out their duties well as deacons will earn a high standing for themselves and be rewarded with great assurance in their work for the faith in Christ Jesus.

The Church and the mystery of the spiritual life

14 At the moment of writing to you, I am 15 hoping that I may be with you soon; ·but in (C3) case I should be delayed, I wanted you to know how people ought to behave in God's family—that is, in the Church of the living God, which upholds the truth and keeps it 16 safe. ·Without any doubt, the mystery of our religion is very deep indeed:

> He was made visible in the flesh,
> attested by the Spirit,
> seen by angels,
> proclaimed to the pagans,
> believed in by the world,
> taken up in glory.

False teachers

4 1 The Spirit has explicitly said that during the last times there will be some who will desert the faith and choose to listen to deceit- (C2) ful spirits and doctrines that come from (C2) 2 the devils; ·and the cause of this is the lies (C2)

told by hypocrites whose consciences are
3 branded as though with a red-hot iron:*a* ·they
will say marriage is forbidden, and lay down
rules about abstaining from foods which God
created to be accepted with thanksgiving by
all who believe and who know the truth.*b*
4 Everything God has created is good, and no
food is to be rejected, provided grace is said
5 for it: ·the word of God and the prayer make
6 it holy. ·If you put all this to the brothers, you
will be a good servant of Christ Jesus and
show that you have really digested the teaching of the faith and the good doctrine which
7 you have always followed. ·Have nothing to
do with godless myths and old wives' tales.
8 Train yourself spiritually. ·"Physical exercises are useful enough, but the usefulness
of spirituality is unlimited, since it holds out
the reward of life here and now and of the
9 future life as well"; ·that is a saying that you
10 can rely on and nobody should doubt it. ·I
mean that the point of all our toiling and
battling is that we have put our trust in the
living God and he is the savior of the whole
human race but particularly of all believers.
11 This is what you are to enforce in your teaching.
12 Do not let people disregard you because
you are young, but be an example to all the
believers in the way you speak and behave,
and in your love, your faith and your purity.
13 Make use of the time until I arrive by reading
14 to the people, preaching and teaching. ·You
have in you a spiritual gift which was given
to you when the prophets spoke and the body
of elders laid their hands on you; do not let
15 it lie unused. ·Think hard about all this, and
put it into practice, and everyone will be able
16 to see how you are advancing. ·Take great
care about what you do and what you teach;
always do this, and in this way you will save
both yourself and those who listen to you.

Week 1 Day 7
Four C's Reflections
on 1 Timothy 3:1-4:16

1. Jesus, Son of Man and Son of God, in today's meditation, St. Paul writes to Timothy about the kind of men who should govern local Churches. He says they should be exemplary Christians. This only makes sense, inasmuch as those under them would regard their words, attitudes and actions as normative for their own lives.

2. We also should lead exemplary Christian lives, whether or not we regard ourselves as leaders, since our conduct does have an influence on others. Non-Christians and non-practicing Christians, for instance, tend to judge the truth of our professed faith in You, Lord, by the type of lives we lead. So do our children, if we happen to be Christian parents. If our conduct is holy, we shall be attracting others closer to You. All that we do or fail to do has an impact, one way or another, on other people. This is an awesome thought, Lord.

3. Most Sacred Heart of Jesus, may we always be mindful of the importance of our conduct, not only for our own salvation and sanctification but for the salvation and sanctification of others as well.

4. Lord, we noticed St. Paul's injunction that priests (presiding elders) and deacons should be married only once was not demanded of lay people.[44] However, in his First Letter to the Corinthians he does encourage Christians, if at all possible, to remain single so as to be able to serve You and Your Church with their undivided attention and charity.[45]

5. Today in many of the Catholic Churches of the East, married men are permitted to become priests and deacons, but they may not remarry if they become widowed. And the same rule applies to married deacons of the Catholic Church in the West. Thus by remaining unmarried, they set an example for the unmarried people whom they serve. *For more on celibate and married clergy, see "The Catholic Catechism," pp. 530-531.)*

6. Lord, we noted with interest St. Paul's instruction that a Christian leader must be able to manage his family well.[46] Parents today, especially, know how difficult this is with so many pressures outside the home which tend to destroy family unity by leading children astray.

7. Jesus, Mary and Joseph, always be the guardians and protectors of our families. And

may parents, who also are subject to outside pressures and allurements, be increasingly aware of the grave responsibilities they have for loving one another unselfishly, and for raising and educating their children according to Christian principles.

8. Jesus, we were pleased to read St. Paul's insistence that everything You, the Father, and the Holy Spirit have created is good in itself. Food, for example, is not evil, and all food may be eaten. "provided grace is said for it: (for) the word of God and prayer make it holy."(47) *(The Church's days of fasting and abstinence are penitential in nature and in no way imply that food is evil. Furthermore, when food is said to be holy it means that it is dedicted to God's service, but unlike human holiness, it does not imply a moral character. See also "The Catholic Catechism," pp. 555-556.)*

9. We see from St. Paul's words, Lord, that grace at meals is an ancient practice. And the Church today encourages us to say grace at

101

our meals. Grace said together as a family can focus mealtime discussions on spiritual and charitable topics and serve to promote family holiness.

10. Lord, may we strive to eat more often together as families. May these occasions become means of uniting us with one another and with You. Just as in a more profound way, participation at the Holy Eucharist serves to unite the family of the whole Church with You.

11. Jesus, in chapter four of today's Scripture reading, St. Paul says You are "the savior of the whole human race but particularly of all believers."[48] This also corresponds to his teaching in chapter two, where he wrote that You want:

12. "...everyone to be saved and reach full knowledge of the truth. For there is only one God, and there is only one mediator between God and mankind, himself a man, Christ Jesus, who sacrificed himself as a ransom for them all."[40]

13. Here, Lord, we see clearly that You have sacrificed Yourself for every human being, no matter how evil some may be. This fact gives us unworthy sinners hope. It also serves to remind those who now accept You with confidence and charity that they are called to be Your representatives in reaching out to sinners who do not yet know or accept You. For You have also died and risen for them. As St. Paul has written elsewhere:

14. "But they will not ask his help unless they believe in him, and they will not believe in him unless they have heard of him, and they will not hear of him unless they get a preacher, and they will never have a preacher unless one is sent."[50]

15. Most Sacred Heart of Jesus, something just came to mind; a moment ago we noted St. Paul said You were the Savior "of the whole human race, but particularly of all believers." But he certainly did not mean that You do not love nor want to save the non-believers as well. What he meant, of course, was that believers have taken the first active steps towards receiving You as their Savior and therefore of experiencing Your saving graces. Whereas those who have never believed in You, have not experienced the fullness of Your saving grace, and often through no fault of their own.

16. Lord Jesus, our only Savior, impress upon us the grave responsibility of presenting the Good News of salvation to others. In charity may we always pray for those who do not presently accept You and Your Catholic Church. And may we have the courage, knowledge and love to share this Good News verbally with them whenever suitable opportunities arise.

17. Finally, Lord, the following words of St. Paul to St. Timothy seem especially appropriate here. "Take great care about what you do and what you teach; always do this, and in this way you will save both your-

self and those who listen to you."[51]

18. Jesus, may our thoughts, words and deeds always reflect You in our lives, thereby attracting many to Your Kingdom. Amen.

Try to read these Scripture passages and meditations in a reflective manner every day. The Holy Spirit will reveal more insights to you each time you do so.

Please read and meditate on Chapter X, Paragraphs 72 to 78 of "Peaceful Seed Living," Volume II.

WEEK 2 DAY 1
1 Timothy 5:1-25

Pastoral practice

5 Do not speak harshly to a man older than yourself, but advise him as you would your own father; treat the younger men as ² brothers ·and older women as you would your mother. Always treat young women with propriety, as if they were sisters.

Widows

3 Be considerate to widows; I mean those ⁴ who are truly widows. ·If a widow has children or grandchildren, they are to learn first of all to do their duty to their own families and repay their debt to their parents, because ⁵ this is what pleases God. ·But a woman who is really widowed and left without anybody can give herself up to God and consecrate all her days and nights to petitions and prayer.

6 The one who thinks only of pleasure is al⁷ ready dead while she is still alive: ·remind them of all this, too, so that their lives may ⁸ be blameless. ·Anyone who does not look after his own relations, especially if they are living with him, has rejected the faith and is worse than an unbeliever.

9 Enrollment as a widow is permissible only for a woman at least sixty years old who has ¹⁰ had only one husband. ·She must be a woman known for her good works and for the way in which she has brought up her children, shown hospitality to strangers and washed the saints' feet, helped people who are in trouble and been active in all kinds of good ¹¹ work. ·Do not accept young widows because if their natural desires get stronger than their dedication to Christ, they want to marry

12 again, ·and then people condemn them for being unfaithful to their original promise.
13 Besides, they learn how to be idle and go round from house to house; and then, not merely idle, they learn to be gossips and meddlers in other people's affairs, and to chatter when they would be better keeping quiet.
14 I think it is best for young widows to marry again and have children and a home to look after, and not give the enemy any chance to
15 raise a scandal about them; ·there are already
16 some who have left us to follow Satan. ·If a Christian woman has widowed relatives, she should support them and not make the Church bear the expense but enable it to support those who are genuinely widows.

The elders

17 The elders who do their work well while they are in charge are to be given double consideration, especially those who are assid-
18 uous in preaching and teaching. ·As scripture says: *You must not muzzle an ox when it is treading out the corn;*[a] and again: *The worker*

19 *deserves his pay.*[b] •Never accept any accusation brought against an elder unless it is sup-
20 ported *by two or three witnesses.* •If any of them are at fault, reprimand them publicly, (C2)(C3)
21 as a warning to the rest. •Before God, and before Jesus Christ and the angels he has chosen, I put it to you as a duty to keep these rules impartially and never to be influenced
22 by favoritism. •Do not be too quick to lay hands on any man, and never make yourself an accomplice in anybody else's sin; keep yourself pure. (C2)(C2)(C2)

23   You should give up drinking only water and have a little wine for the sake of your digestion and the frequent bouts of illness that you have.

24   The faults of some people are obvious long before anyone makes any complaint about them, while others have faults that are not (C2)(C2)
25 discovered until afterward. •In the same way, the good that people do can be obvious; but (C3) even when it is not, it cannot be hidden for ever.

Week 2 Day 1
Four C's Reflections
on 1 Timothy 5:1-25

1. Jesus, our meditation for today is filled with practical advice much needed today.

2. It was not too many years ago that St. Paul's teaching that older people should be treated with respect and charity was widely heeded.[52] Now, however, older people are often treated disrespectfully and uncharitably.

3. Sometimes no disrespectful words are spoken, but the elderly are treated disrespectfully by being simply ignored. We remember, for example, the case of a widow who was placed in a nursing home by her son. He then proceeded to move himself and his family into her house rent-free. Nevertheless, the son rarely visited his mother, even though the nursing home was only a few blocks away.

4. Older neighborhoods often have elderly people who are very lonely. This is especially sad when they are living apart from their children and from former friends and associates.

5. We know from experience that some nursing homes are hardly better than prisons for senior citizens. Laughter and joy are not the rule in these institutions, and offensive smells often fill the rooms and corridors. Moreover, unlike most hospitals, visitors are few.

6. Conditions such as these, Lord, coupled with the high cost of nursing care, has led to a clamor by some for euthanasia instead of truly humane Christian treatment. If we were either passively or actively to support euthanasia, we would be guilty of fostering murder. St. Paul himself condemned euthanasia of one's parents when he noted that laws exist, not for those who are good, but actually "for criminals and revolutionaries, for the irreligious and the wicked . . . for people who kill their fathers or mothers . . ."[53]

7. Jesus, there is a tendency in our society to think that money alone is sufficient for the needs of the elderly. Actually what is more needed is our personal contact with them, and our words of kindness, joy and respect.

8. Furthermore, there is the notion that the elderly like to live alone or away from those younger than themselves. This is sometimes true, but most of them would really like to be in frequent contact with younger people, especially with children.

9. We recall an occasion when a baby was taken into a nursing home to visit his dying great-grandmother. All up and down the corridor to her room were residents in wheel chairs reaching out to hold and kiss the infant, while broad smiles appeared on their faces.

10. Most Sacred Heart of Jesus, many young people today entertain the notion that elderly people are "know-nothings" or that what they know has no meaning for our

times. Such an attitude contradicts the verdict of human history. With rare exceptions senior citizens have been honored and respected, not only for their knowledge gained over a lifetime, but especially for their wisdom.

11. Lord, help us to be more mindful and considerate of our senior citizens. May we visit them more often, and constantly pray for them, remembering that most of us shall one day be old, and we will certainly want to be treated charitably.

12. St. Paul also teaches that older Christians should treat younger men as brothers and "young women with propriety, as if they were sisters."(54) Lord, Jesus, there is a tendency today by some to exploit younger men and boys sexually, and to introduce them to various types of drugs. Thankfully, this is not very general and we pray that it will never be. But there is an alarming trend towards the sexual

exploitation of young women and girls by older and younger men.

13. Lord, this is not the place to dwell on why this is wrong. For now, let us simply accept St. Paul's teaching in this regard, since it is also Your teaching.

14. Young women and girls, as well as older women, should be treated with respect and not as objects of self-gratification. To so exploit them is contrary to seed-charity and therefore is sinful.

15. Older and younger men should treat young women as if they were sisters. Or we might add, as if they were the Blessed Virgin Mary herself. If they were treated in this way, God would bless our society with happier and holier marriages and families.

16. Lord, Jesus, may we who profess to be Christians treat others with respect and charity since they too are created in Your image and likeness. For those who are

tempted to commit sexual sins, strengthen their wills by Your grace and teach them self-control. May they always turn to Your Immaculate Mother and to St. Joseph, her most chaste spouse, whose great help in this regard has been witnessed for centuries. *(See "The Catholic Catechism," pp. 353-356 for the Catholic teaching on sexual pleasure.)*

17. Lord, St. Paul has some excellent advice for lonely widows. He says that they can give themselves to God and consecrate all their "days and nights to petitions and prayer."[55] These words are applicable to all the lonely elderly, not only to lonely widows.

18. What a marvelous thought! If only this were to be suggested to all senior citizens who experienced great loneliness. What great good would result if large numbers of them were to dedicate themselves to a life of prayer. Their loneliness would be relieved by the awareness of Your comforting presence, and You would be reaching the needs of others through their constant intercessions.

19. Lord, we also saw in today's Scripture reading that St. Paul cautioned St. Timothy against favoritism.[56] This is sound advice and reflects his teaching elsewhere that "God has no favorites."[57] May we always treat everyone charitably and impartially, since to "play favorites" is a sin against both charity and justice.

20. Jesus, St. Paul also reminded St. Timothy that the person "who thinks only of

pleasure is already dead while she is still alive."[58] This teaching is especially appropriate today, when so many are pleasure-oriented and consequently selfish. In fact, we are meant to be oriented primarily to God, the Creator and only true Source of lasting happiness.

21. A pleasure-oriented person is never really happy and is cut off from Your friendship, since You demand self-sacrifice. Consequently they are, as St. Paul says, dead, that is, spiritually dead.

22. Most Merciful Savior, through our prayers and good examples, help those who live mainly for the bitterness of earthly pleasures. May our sacrifices help to free them from such cruel slavery. Amen.

Try to read these Scripture passages and meditations in a reflective manner every day. The Holy Spirit will reveal more insights to you each time you do so.

Please read and meditate on Chapter X, Paragraphs 79 to 92 of "Peaceful Seed Living," Volume II.

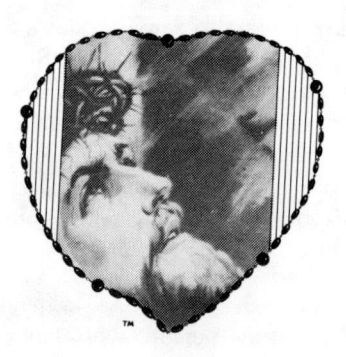

WEEK 2 DAY 2
1 Timothy 6:1-21

Slaves

1 All slaves "under the yoke" must have unqualified respect for their masters, so that the name of God and our teaching are not brought into disrepute. ·Slaves whose masters are believers are not to think any the less of them because they are brothers; on the contrary, they should serve them all the better, since those who have the benefit of their services are believers and dear to God.

The true teacher and the false teacher

This is what you are to teach them to believe and persuade them to do. ·Anyone who teaches anything different, and does not keep to the sound teaching which is that of our Lord Jesus Christ, the doctrine which is in accordance with true religion, ·is simply ignorant and must be full of self-conceit—with a craze for questioning everything and arguing about words. All that can come of this is jealousy, contention, abuse and wicked mistrust of one another; ·and unending disputes by people who are neither rational nor informed and imagine that religion is a way of making a profit. ·Religion, of course, does bring large profits, but only to those who are content with what they have. ·We brought nothing into the world, and we can take nothing out of it; ·but as long as we have food and clothing, let us be content with that. People who long to be rich are a prey to temptation; they get trapped into all sorts of foolish and dangerous ambitions which

eventually plunge them into ruin and destruc-
10 tion. •"The love of money is the root of all evils," and there are some who, pursuing it, have wandered away from the faith, and so given their souls any number of fatal wounds.

Timothy's vocation recalled

11 But, as a man dedicated to God, you must avoid all that. You must aim to be saintly and religious, filled with faith and love, patient
12 and gentle. •Fight the good fight of the faith and win for yourself the eternal life to which you were called when you made your profession and spoke up for the truth in front of
13 many witnesses. •Now, before God the source of all life and before Jesus Christ, who spoke up as a witness for the truth in front
14 of Pontius Pilate, I put to you the duty •of doing all that you have been told, with no faults or failures, until the Appearing of our Lord Jesus Christ,

15 who at the due time will be revealed
by God, the blessed and only Ruler of all,
the King of kings and the Lord of lords,
16 who alone is immortal,
whose home is in inaccessible light,
whom no man has seen and no man is able
  to see:
to him be honor and everlasting power.
Amen.

Rich Christians

17 Warn those who are rich in this world's goods that they are not to look down on other people; and not to set their hopes on money, which is untrustworthy, but on God who, out of his riches, gives us all that we need for our
18 happiness. •Tell them that they are to do good, and be rich in good works, to be gener-
19 ous and willing to share—•this is the way

they can save up a good capital sum for the future if they want to make sure of the only life that is real.

Final warning and conclusion

20 My dear Timothy, take great care of all (C3) that has been entrusted to you. Have nothing to do with the pointless philosophical discus- (C2) sions and antagonistic beliefs of the "knowl-
21 edge" which is not knowledge at all; ·by adopting this, some have gone right away (C2) from the faith. Grace be with you.

Week 2 Day 2
Four C's Reflections
on 1 Timothy 6:1-21

1. Most Sacred Heart of Jesus, we observed in today's reading that St. Paul emphasized once more the importance of teaching only Your doctrine.[59] Unfortunately, time and again, from the first century until now, there have been individuals within the Catholic Church itself who have falsified Your teaching. In our own day, for example, there are those who promote the use of artificial birth control and maintain that no one commits mortal sin who does not consciously and deliberately reject God. *(For a thorough presentation on contraception, see pp. 367-381 of "The Catholic Catechism." See also the entry "Fundamental Option" in the "Modern Catholic Dictionary" pp. 222-224 for a discussion of the latter notion.)*

2. Surely, Lord, we do not always understand Your doctrines, but since You teach them we must trust in You and believe them for the salvation of our immortal souls. How many things, for instance, in the field of science, we do not understand, yet this does not mean they are not true. We have in mind such things as the way television, computers, or atomic fission and fusion work, or the way a living organism grows and develops. If we do not understand such things as these, how much more must this be true of things that are spiritual and moral in nature, which are not subject to the scrutiny of the laboratory. This reminds us of Your words to Nicodemus "I tell

you most solemnly, unless a man is born through water and the Spirit, he cannot enter the kingdom of God: what is born of the flesh is flesh; what is born of the Spirit is spirit. Do not be surprised when I say: You must be born from above. The wind blows wherever it pleases; you hear its sound, but you cannot tell where it comes from or where it is going. That is how it is with all who are born of the Spirit. 'How can that be possible?' asked Nicodemus. 'You, a teacher in Israel, and you do not know these things!' replied Jesus. 'I tell you most solemnly, we speak only about what we know and witness only to what we have seen and yet you people reject our evidence. If you do not believe me when I speak about things in this world, how are you going to believe me when I speak to you about heavenly things.' "(60)

3. If we stop to think about it, Lord, much of the knowledge we accept as true in this life is taken on faith in the person or persons who

taught it, and not from our own study and verification. In light of this, it is not at all unreasonable to accept as true all that You, Who are God, taught Your Apostles and committed to the safe-keeping of the Church of Rome. *(For the teaching of the Second Vatican Council on the place of the Church of Rome in Christianity, see p. 213 of "The Catholic Catechism.")*

4. Another thing which is falsely taught by some today is that we need accept as true doctrine only that which has been infallibly defined by the Pope or by an ecumenical council under the Pope.

5. This position is far from the truth. Infallible definitions in matters of faith and morals are normally given only in rare instances when there is widespread and persistent confusion on some point of doctrine. Infallible definitions are rendered in order to settle the confusion for all time. On the other hand, there are a multitude of doctrines which are true (inerrant) and will always remain true, but have never been expressly defined. Such things, for example, are the duty to love God above all else and our neighbor as ourselves, and affirmations that murder, abortion and artificial birth control are evil, and the fact that the Blessed Virgin Mary loves You with a pure maternal love. These truths are to be accepted with the gift of faith. *(For more on doctrinal infallibility, see "The Catholic Catechism," pp. 224-233.)*

6. Lord, by the power of Your Holy Spirit, may we always believe all You teach, so that

we may have knowledge of You and Your will for us.

7. Moreover, while reading our Scripture meditation for today, our eyes focused on St. Paul's teaching that we should be satisfied with the necessities of life and not long for wealth.

8. "We brought nothing into the world, and we can take nothing out of it; but as long as we have food and clothing, let us be content with that. People who long to be rich are prey to temptations; they get trapped into all sorts of foolish and dangerous ambitions which eventually plunge them into ruin and destruction. 'The love of money is the root of all evils' and there are some who, pursuing it, have wandered away from the faith, and so given their souls any number of fatal wounds."[61]

9. Basically, Lord, You are telling us through St. Paul, that avarice or greed is a form of self-centeredness, as opposed to God-centeredness. It leads to all types of sins which can only bring unhappiness instead of the hoped for happiness.

10. Essentially, greed is a form of idolatry. That is, it is a false god which people worship in order to please themselves rather than pleasing God. "That is why you must kill everything in you that belongs only to earthly life: fornication, impurity, guilty passion, evil desires and especially greed, which is the same thing as worshipping a false god; all this is the sort of behavior that makes God angry."(62)

11. Again, St. Paul writes to St. Timothy:

12. "Warn those who are rich in this world's goods that they are not to look down on other people; and not to set their hopes on money,

which is untrustworthy, but on God who, out of his riches, gives us all that we need for our happiness."[63] Jesus, this corresponds with what was recorded of You in St. Luke's Gospel. "Watch, and be on your guard against avarice of any kind, for a man's life is not made secure by what he owns, even when he has more than he needs."[64]

13. Lord, we know that You and St. Paul are not telling us that money is evil. In itself, it is capable of doing a great deal of good. Nevertheless, it is not the Source of all goodness and happiness. Only You, the Father and the Holy Spirit are that. Yet, in our materialistic culture, there is a tendency to believe money will solve all of our problems. Therefore, it is not surprising that greed, one of the seven deadly sins, is so prevalent. *(The seven deadly or capital sins are pride, greed or avarice, lust, envy, gluttony, anger and laziness or sloth. For a discussion of these see p. 81 of "The Modern Catholic Dictionary.")*

14. This is unfortunate, even tragic, since it is only those, whether rich or poor, who place You first in their lives and look to You rather than to wealth to supply their basic needs, that are really happy.

15. St. Paul is a prime example of one who had very little in the way of material wealth, yet was constantly at peace with himself because of Your grace. Then there was King St. Louis of France (1214-1270), who was not poor, yet he placed his confidence in You rather than in his riches and found great

peace also. Moreover, he used his wealth to help those who lacked the material necessities of life.

16. St. Louis may well have taken the following words of St. Paul as normative regarding the use of his riches.

17. "Tell them (the rich) that they are to do good, and be rich in good works, to be generous and willing to share — this is the way they can save up a good capital sum for the future if they want to make sure of the only life that is real."[65]

18. Most Sacred Heart of Jesus, help us not to place too much reliance on money. Guard us from greed. Inspire us to be generous, especially towards the needy. And may we place our confidence primarily on You Who promised if we would first seek God's Kingdom and His righteousness, all our needs would be met.[66] Amen.

Try to read these Scripture passages and meditations in a reflective manner every day. The Holy Spirit will reveal more insights to you each time you do so.

Please read and meditate on Chapter XI, Paragraphs 1 to 20 of "Peaceful Seed Living," Volume II.

WEEK 2 DAY 3
2 Timothy 1:1-18

2 Timothy

THE SECOND LETTER FROM PAUL TO TIMOTHY

Greeting and thanksgiving

1 From Paul, appointed by God to be an apostle of Christ Jesus in his design to
2 promise life in Christ Jesus; •to Timothy, dear child of mine, wishing you grace, mercy (C3) and peace from God the Father and from Christ Jesus our Lord.
3 Night and day I thank God, keeping my (C3) conscience clear and remembering my duty (C2) to him as my ancestors did, and always I remember you in my prayers; I remember (C3)
4 your tears •and long to see you again to com- (C3)
5 plete my happiness. •Then I am reminded of the sincere faith which you have; it came first (C1) to live in your grandmother Lois, and your mother Eunice, and I have no doubt that it is the same faith in you as well. (C1)

(C1)

The gifts that Timothy has received

6 That is why I am reminding you now to fan into a flame the gift that God gave you when
7 I laid my hands on you. •God's gift was not a spirit of timidity, but the Spirit of power,

8 and love, and self-control. ·So you are never to be ashamed of witnessing to the Lord, or ashamed of me for being his prisoner; but with me, bear the hardships for the sake of the Good News, relying on the power of God
9 who has saved us and called us to be holy— not because of anything we ourselves have done but for his own purpose and by his own grace. This grace had already been granted to us, in Christ Jesus, before the beginning
10 of time, ·but it has only been revealed by the Appearing of our savior Christ Jesus. He abolished death, and he has proclaimed life and immortality through the Good News;
11 and I have been named its herald, its apostle and its teacher.

12   It is only on account of this that I am experiencing fresh hardships here now;*a* but I have not lost confidence, because I know who it is that I have put my trust in, and I have no doubt at all that he is able to take care of all that I have entrusted to him until that Day.

13   Keep as your pattern the sound teaching you have heard from me, in the faith and love
14 that are in Christ Jesus. ·You have been trusted to look after something precious; guard it with the help of the Holy Spirit who lives in us.

15   As you know, Phygelus and Hermogenes and all the others from Asia refuse to have
16 anything more to do with me. ·I hope the Lord will be kind to all the family of Onesiphorus, because he has often been a comfort to me and has never been ashamed of
17 my chains. ·On the contrary, as soon as he reached Rome, he really searched hard for
18 me and found out where I was. ·May it be the Lord's will that he shall find the Lord's mercy on that Day. You know better than anyone else how much he helped me at Ephesus.

125

Week 2 Day 3
Four C's Reflections
on 2 Timothy 1:1-18

1. Most Sacred Heart of Jesus, in St. Paul's Second Letter to Timothy, he writes, "Night and day, I thank God, keeping my conscience clear..."[67] We imagine by the time he wrote this, St. Paul was able to keep his conscience free from most sins, because he had become "addicted" to a life of Christian virtue through his constant cooperation with Your graces.[68] *(Be sure to read the introductory remarks about 2 Timothy beginning on p. 27 of this book.)*

2. Most of us, however, are far from that stage of spiritual growth where we keep our consciences entirely free from sin. Nonetheless, we are obliged as Your friends and followers to keep our consciences pure. But how are we to do this, Lord, since we fall into sin so often?

3. In the first place, Your Church teaches us to examine our consciences frequently, confess our sins with true sorrow, and ask God to forgive us. In the case of grave or mortal sins we should tell God we are sorry immediately after committing them, and then, as soon as possible, avail ourselves of priestly absolution in the sacrament of Penance.

4. Moreover, Your Church encourages us to use this healing sacrament for the confession of venial sins, since through sacramental Confession You give us an increase of grace and strengthen our wills. Those who receive Holy Communion frequently and properly will also receive abundant graces to free themselves from venial sins. *(See "The Catholic Catechism," p. 496 for a statement on the importance of the frequent reception of the sacrament of Penance.)*

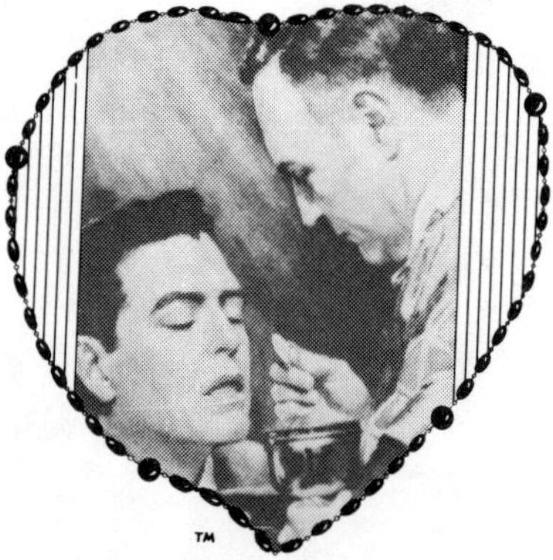

5. Secondly, in order to acquire a clear conscience, Jesus, we must use Your grace and strive to resist temptations to sin, as St. Paul did. By continuous striving, we shall notice we are sinning less frequently over a period of weeks, months and years. Provided we make the effort, we can even stop committing certain habitual sins entirely.

6. Lord, may Your Holy Spirit constantly remind us of the seriousness of sin and how it offends You and harms the whole world, as well as our own souls. May He also inspire us to examine our consciences daily, to repent of our sins with a deep sorrow and to remain steadfast in virtue. And through fervent prayer and the frequent reception of the sacraments may we receive grace to strengthen our resolve against ever-present temptations.

7. Jesus, in today's meditation, St. Paul mentions that he is enduring still more hardships. Nevertheless, he says:

8. "I have not lost confidence, because I know who it is that I have put my trust in, and I have no doubt at all that he is able to take care of all that I have entrusted to him until that Day."[69]

9. Lord, we, like St. Paul, must learn to place our confidence entirely in You, believing You will see us safely through every hardship and through every crisis as long as we remain in Your friendship.

10. The hardships we must endure are

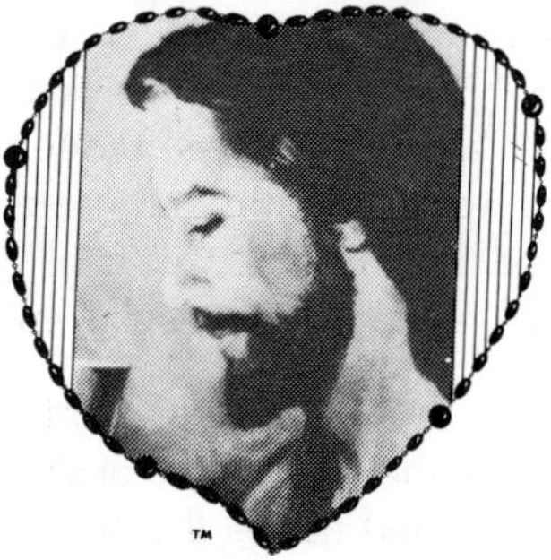

opportunities to know You better, as we draw closer to You through prayer and the sacraments to seek Your comfort and support. And they are opportunities to grow in holiness as we learn to cope with them in a Christian manner. On the other hand, hardships can also tempt us to lose confidence in You and to look elsewhere for solace, thus leading us further away from You and holiness. Many people in fact blame You, Who are God, for their problems. Others view hardships as evidence You do not care for them. And still others see them as evidence that You do not exist. Thus, they have an excuse not to pray to You nor to worship You, and to lead an immoral life should they wish to do so.

11. Actually, the hardships, crises and trials we encounter are not of Your positive making. They are due to original and actual sin and their effects. In other words, they are the result of the abuse of human freedom, as

well as the perverse will of demons. *(For a discussion on original sin, read pp. 99-102 of "The Catholic Catechism.")*

12. It is true that You permit hardships, crises and trials to exist. But to do otherwise would be a denial of full freedom to ourselves and angels. On the other hand, You would never permit them, if evil could not be turned into good. The way of sanctity, for instance, is paved with hardships. And You Yourself, Lord, Who were, and are, completely without sin, deserving neither sorrows nor trials, obtained our redemption by Your patient endurance and Your complete trust and love of the Father. *(For more on fallen angels, see "The Catholic Catechism, pp. 83-90.)*

13. Trials, sorrows and hardships then, Lord, are opportunities to increase our faith and hope in You and to grow in charity. They are not evidence of Your lack of concern for us, but rather of Your providential love since they are means of bringing us ever closer to You, and thus to true peace and happiness. And most certainly they are not evidence of Your supposed non-existence. To hold such a position is truly absurd. It is like saying that since children quarrel, fight, and get ill, they could not possibly have parents.

14. Finally, Jesus, we would like to comment on St. Paul's statement to Timothy that he must "never to be ashamed of witnessing to the Lord..."[70] This feeling of shame a person has regarding You and Your words of salvation may well be largely due to

diabolical inspirations. Why should St. Timothy or anyone else who has experienced Your presence and activity in their lives be ashamed of You? Nevertheless, we cannot deny that we are sometimes tempted to feel this way. Moreover, You Yourself anticipated this when You said, "For if anyone is ashamed of me and of my words, of him the Son of Man will be ashamed when he comes in his own glory and in the glory of the Father and the holy angels."[71]

15. Lord, what is basically at issue here is our self-love as opposed to our love for You and our desire for the salvation of others. We are often ashamed to declare Your goodness and mercy because we are afraid we will be laughed at or rejected. So in the last analysis we must ask ourselves what is more important; our desire for acceptance by others who cannot save us, or by You Who can? Furthermore, while many may reject us because of our love for You and the Gospel, there will be those also who will not reject us or Your Gospel. And if we do not share You and the Good News with others, who will? Actually, it is selfish of us to accept You and all You have to offer us, and at the same time refuse to share You with others.

16. Lord Jesus, give us such love for You and Your Gospel and for others, that we will fearlessly speak out on Your behalf before our friends and acquaintances, so that they too may share in the salvation You have earned for all of us. And constantly remind us that if we do not share You with others, we risk

losing our own salvation, just as the man who lost the talent which had been entrusted to him because he hid it in the ground.[(72)] Amen.

Try to read these Scripture passages and meditations in a reflective manner every day. The Holy Spirit will reveal more insights to you each time you do so.

Please read and meditate on Chapter XI, Paragraphs 21 to 22, and Chapter XII, Introduction and Paragraphs 1 to 4, Chapter XIV, "Peaceful Seed Living," Volume II.

WEEK 2 DAY 4
2 Timothy 2:1-26

How Timothy should face hardships

2 1 Accept the strength, my dear son, that comes from the grace of Christ Jesus. (C3)

2 You have heard everything that I teach in public; hand it on to reliable people so that they in turn will be able to teach others. (C3)

3 Put up with your share of difficulties, like (C3)
4 a good soldier of Christ Jesus. ·In the army, no soldier gets himself mixed up in civilian life, because he must be at the disposal of the (C4)
5 man who enlisted him; ·or take an athlete —he cannot win any crown unless he has
6 kept all the rules of the contest; ·and again, it is the working farmer who has the first
7 claim on any crop that is harvested. ·Think over what I have said, and the Lord will show you how to understand it all.

8 Remember the Good News that I carry, "Jesus Christ risen from the dead, sprung
9 from the race of David"; ·it is on account of this that I have my own hardships to bear, even to being chained like a criminal—but (C3) (C4)
10 they cannot chain up God's news. ·So I bear it all for the sake of those who are chosen, so that in the end they may have the salvation that is in Christ Jesus and the eternal glory that comes with it. (C4) (C3)

11 Here is a saying that you can rely on:

If we have died with him, then we shall live with him. (C3)

12 If we hold firm, then we shall reign with him. (C4)
If we disown him, then he will disown us. (C2)
13 We may be unfaithful, but he is always faithful, (C2)
for he cannot disown his own self.

The struggle against the immediate danger from false teachers

14 Remind them of this; and tell them in the name of God that there is to be no wrangling about words: all that this ever achieves is the
15 destruction of those who are listening. ·Do all you can to present yourself in front of God as a man who has come through his trials, and a man who has no cause to be ashamed of his life's work and has kept a straight course
16 with the message of the truth. ·Have nothing to do with pointless philosophical discussions—they only lead further and further
17 away from true religion. ·Talk of this kind corrodes like gangrene, as in the case of
18 Hymenaeus and Philetus, ·the men who have gone right away from the truth and claim that the resurrection has already taken place. Some people's faith cannot stand up to them.

19 However, God's solid foundation stone is still in position, and this is the inscription on it: *"The Lord knows those who are his own"*[a] and "All who *call on the name of the Lord*[b] must avoid sin."

20 Not all the dishes in a large house are made of gold and silver; some are made of wood or earthenware: some are kept for special

occasions and others are for ordinary pur-
21 poses. •Now, to avoid these faults that I am speaking about is the way for anyone to become a vessel for special occasions, fit for the Master himself to use, and kept ready for any good work.
22 Instead of giving in to your impulses like a young man, fasten your attention on holiness, faith, love and peace, in union with all those who call on the Lord with pure minds.
23 Avoid these futile and silly speculations, understanding that they only give rise to quar-
24 rels; •and a servant of the Lord is not to engage in quarrels, but has to be kind to ev-
25 eryone, a good teacher, and patient. •He has to be gentle when he corrects people who dispute what he says, never forgetting that God may give them a change of mind so that
26 they recognize the truth and •come to their senses, once out of the trap where the devil caught them and kept them enslaved.

Week 2 Day 4
Four C's Reflections
on 2 Timothy 2:1-26

1. Lord, we saw in today's Scripture reading that St. Paul continued to speak about trials and hardships which happen to Your true friends and disciples. Help us to accept them since they represent the cross which You said we must take and carry each day. Furthermore, as we observed yesterday, we can look at trials and hardships as opportunities to know You better and to grow in holiness. [73]

2. Jesus, in today's meditation, St. Paul also mentioned the strength we receive from Your grace so we will be able to bear our crosses. Writing to Timothy, he said, "Accept the strength, my dear son, that comes from the grace of Christ Jesus."[74]

3. We know from the Church's Faith, Lord, that You will give us strength to endure hardships and to do Your will in general. Yet, when we are actually faced with some particular difficulty we are often tempted to give in rather than call for Your help, or make use of the grace that is already within us. Too often we act as if we were alone and confronted with an intolerable burden.

4. Dear Lord, You always supply us with the strength to do Your will, at least by giving us the grace to pray for the strength that we need. However, we must then cooperate with You by exercising our will power. Yet, as

many of us know from experience, even when we cooperate with Your grace to do some particularly difficult thing, it is still often not easy. But if we persevere we will succeed. And in the case of some habitual sin, the more we persevere, usually the easier it becomes to resist with each successive victory. Moreover, these victories in turn give us confidence to battle succesfully with other hardships which we will surely encounter.

5. Lord, St. Paul also told St. Timothy to teach the Gospel to reliable people who would then be able to teach others.[74] Although St. Paul did not especially have parents in mind, this passage can be a reminder to them that they are the ones primarily responsible for the education of their children, including their religious education. How vital it is, Jesus, for parents to take this God-given vocation seriously, so the Church may be strengthened and society flourish in accordance with Your eternal truths.

6. The parents' responsibility to educate their children is so important that the Second Vatican Council saw fit to stress it in the following words:

7. "It is the parents who have given life to their children, on them lies the greatest obligation of educating their family. They must therefore be recognized as being primarily and principally responsible for their education. The role of parents in education is of such importance that it is almost impossible to provide an adequate substitute. It is

therefore the duty of parents to create a family atmosphere inspired by love and devotion to God and their fellow man which will promote an integrated, personal and social education of their children. The family is therefore the principal school of the social virtues which are necessary to every society. It is therefore above all in the Christian family, inspired by the grace and responsibility of the sacrament of Matrimony, that children should be taught to know and worship God and to love their neighbors, in accordance with the faith which they have received in earliest infancy in the sacrament of Baptism. In it, also, they will have their first experience of a well-balanced human society and of the Church. Finally, it is through the family that they are gradually initiated into association with their fellow men in civil life and as members of people of God. Parents should, therefore, appreciate how important a role the truly Christian family plays in the life and progress of the whole people of God." *(Austin Flannery, O.P., (Ed.), "Vatican Council II," pp. 728-729. See also "The Catholic Catechism," pp. 33-34.)*

8. Lord, we are thankful that the Fathers of the Second Vatican Council reminded parents of their duty to educate their children in the Catholic Faith. They really needed this reminder since they have become so accustomed to letting professionals and volunteers take over the major portion of this task. Although these people can be of immense service in helping parents carry out their duty, they must not expect them, or even let them, take over the primary responsibility. Therefore, in the area of Faith, many parents should be more diligent in teaching it at home, and in helping teachers, administrators and others in the selection of materials which fully reflect Catholic doctrine. Moreover, they should not be afraid to find out whether professionals and others in the field of Catholic education fully subscribe to the Catholic Faith.

9. This can be done most easily by examining their children's textbooks, being on the outlook for doctrinal errors, omissions of primary teachings such as those contained in the Church's creeds, and for ambiguous or unclear language.

10. Jesus, Mary and Joseph, protect our families from all physical and spiritual harm. And we thank You for all You have already

done for us. Also, may we always look to You as the model of perfect living, and never fail to invoke Your protection in our moments of need.

11. Finally, Jesus, in our meditation for today, we dwelt on the following statement concerning You.

12. "If we have died with him, then we shall live with him. If we hold firm, then we shall reign with him. If we disown him, then he will disown us. We may be unfaithful, but he is always faithful, for he cannot disown his own self."[76]

13. In other words, St. Paul is saying that if we, through Your grace, have died to sinfulness, we shall live in Your friendship, even in this life. And if we remain in Your friendship, until the moment of death, we shall reign with You in eternity.

14. But we must not presume that we will always remain in Your friendship, no matter what. Not at all! If we commit mortal sin we in effect disown You. On the other hand, You Who thankfully are always faithful, will never initiate the break in our relationship with You. Furthermore, You always plead with us to return to You should we choose to reject You through our sins.

15. Lord, help us never to reject You and endanger our eternal salvation. But if we should be so foolish as to do so, inspire us to confess our sins sincerely in the sacrament of Penance, so we may return to Your friendship and live with You forever. Amen.

Try to read these Scripture passages and meditations in a reflective manner every day. The Holy Spirit will reveal more insights to you each time you do so.

Please read and meditate on Chapter XII, Paragraphs 15 to 34 of "Peaceful Seed Living," Volume II.

WEEK 2 DAY 5
2 Timothy 3:1-4:22

The dangers of the last days

1 3 You may be quite sure that in the last days there are going to be some difficult times.
2 People will be self-centered and grasping; boastful, arrogant and rude; disobedient to
3 their parents, ungrateful, irreligious; ·heartless and unappeasable; they will be slanderers, profligates, savages and enemies of
4 everything that is good; ·they will be treacherous and reckless and demented by pride, preferring their own pleasure to God.
5 They will keep up the outward appearance of religion but will have rejected the inner power of it. Have nothing to do with people like that.

6 Of the same kind, too, are those men who insinuate themselves into families in order to get influence over silly women who are obsessed with their sins and follow one craze
7 after another ·in the attempt to educate themselves, but can never come to knowledge of
8 the truth. ·Men like this defy the truth just as Jannes and Jambres defied Moses:[a] their minds are corrupt and their faith spurious.
9 But they will not be able to go on any longer: their foolishness, like that of the other two, must become obvious to everybody.

10 You know, though, what I have taught, how I have lived, what I have aimed at; you know my faith, my patience and my love; my
11 constancy ·and the persecutions and hardships that came to me in places like Antioch, Iconium and Lystra—all the persecutions I have endured; and the Lord has rescued me
12 from every one of them. ·You are well aware, then, that anybody who tries to live in devo-
13 tion to Christ is certain to be attacked; ·while

these wicked impostors will go from bad to worse, deceiving others and deceived themselves.
14 You must keep to what you have been taught and know to be true; remember who
15 your teachers were, ·and how, ever since you were a child, you have known the holy scriptures—from these you can learn the wisdom that leads to salvation through faith in Christ
16 Jesus. ·All scripture is inspired by God and can profitably be used for teaching, for refuting error, for guiding people's lives and
17 teaching them to be holy. ·This is how the man who is dedicated to God becomes fully equipped and ready for any good work.

A solemn charge

1 Before God and before Christ Jesus who is to be judge of the living and the dead, I put this duty to you, in the name of his
2 Appearing and of his kingdom: ·proclaim the message and, welcome or unwelcome, insist on it. Refute falsehood, correct error, call to obedience—but do all with patience and with
3 the intention of teaching. ·The time is sure

to come when, far from being content with sound teaching, people will be avid for the latest novelty and collect themselves a whole series of teachers according to their own ⁴ tastes; ·and then, instead of listening to the ⁵ truth, they will turn to myths. ·Be careful always to choose the right course; be brave under trials; make the preaching of the Good News your life's work, in thoroughgoing service.

Paul in the evening of his life

⁶ As for me, my life is already being poured away as a libation, and the time has come for ⁷ me to be gone. ·I have fought the good fight to the end; I have run the race to the finish; ⁸ I have kept the faith; ·all there is to come now is the crown of righteousness reserved for me, which the Lord, the righteous judge, will give to me on that Day; and not only to me but to all those who have longed for his Appearing.

Final advice

⁹ Do your best to come and see me as soon ¹⁰ as you can. ·As it is, Demas has deserted me for love of this life and gone to Thessalonika, Crescens has gone to Galatia and Titus to ¹¹ Dalmatia; ·only Luke is with me. Get Mark to come and bring him with you; I find him ¹² a useful helper in my work. ·I have sent Ty-¹³ chicus to Ephesus. ·When you come, bring the cloak I left with Carpus in Troas, and the ¹⁴ scrolls, especially the parchment ones. ·Alexander the coppersmith has done me a lot of harm; *the Lord will repay him for what he has* ¹⁵ *done.*ᵃ ·Be on your guard against him yourself, because he has been bitterly contesting everything that we say.

¹⁶ The first time I had to present my defense, there was not a single witness to support me. Every one of them deserted me—may they

17 not be held accountable for it. ·But the Lord stood by me and gave me power, so that through me the whole message might be proclaimed for all the pagans to hear; and so I
18 was *rescued from the lion's mouth.*[b] ·The Lord will rescue me from all evil attempts on me, and bring me safely to his heavenly kingdom. To him be glory for ever and ever. Amen. (C2)

Farewells and final good wishes

19 Greetings to Prisca and Aquila, and the
20 family of Onesiphorus. ·Erastus remained at Corinth, and I left Trophimus ill at Miletus.
21 Do your best to come before the winter.

Greetings to you from Eubulus, Pudens, Linus, Claudia and all the brothers.

22 The Lord be with your spirit. Grace be with you. (C3)

Week 2 Day 5
Four C's Reflections
on 2 Timothy 3:1-4:22

1. Jesus, Our Lord, we observed in today's Scripture lesson St. Paul's admonition to St. Timothy to proclaim the message of the Gospel and to insist on it whether it was welcome or unwelcome. This was to be done even if there was a clamor for deviations from the Catholic Faith.[77]

2. Obviously, if the Faith were to be presented in a deviated form, it would no longer be the message of the Gospel. Consequently those who accepted this counterfeit faith would be led astray and not by the straight path of truth which leads to salvation. In the second place, had St. Timothy misrepresented Your doctrine, he would have been unfaithful to his vocation as a Catholic priest and bishop. He would be representing himself or someone else, but not You, whose priest and bishop he was.

3. With these thoughts in mind, we cannot help but admire Pope Paul VI, who insisted on teaching only Your Catholic doctrine on birth control, in spite of widespread opposition from clergy and laity.

4. Using Pope Paul as an example of fidelity to Your sacred doctrine, teachers of religion, whether at home or elsewhere, must also insist on teaching only Catholic doctrine, omitting nothing that might prove unwelcome to their hearers. By doing so, they will be

performing a true service of seed-charity, both for You and their students.

5. On the other hand, when religion teachers instruct others, they should do so tactfully and patiently, without intending to offend. As St. Paul wrote to St. Timothy, "Refute falsehood, correct error, call to obedience — but do all with patience and with the intention of teaching...be careful always to choose the right course..."[78]

6. Lord, thank You for inspiring St. Paul to write these words since they give us so much comfort. We should teach only sound doctrine. If we do so in a charitable manner, we need not worry about the fact that some might reject Your teaching. After all, there were those who rejected Your teaching while You were proclaiming it on earth. Even Your miracles did not move many of them to accept what You taught.

7. St. Paul rightly understood such people when he said:

8. "The time is sure to come when, far from being content with sound teaching, people will be avid for the latest novelty and collect themselves a whole series of teachers according to their own tastes; and then, instead of listening to the truth, they will turn to myths."[79]

9. Also, Lord, we were struck by St. Paul's description of what living in the "last days" would be like, of which our present times are a part. It certainly sounded familiar. *(While the term "last days" may refer to the time of the Second Coming, it may also refer, as it does here, to that period ushered in by Christ's Crucifixion and Resurrection, which will last until the time of Christ's return at the "Last Day" and the final judgment of mankind.)*

10. "You may be quite sure that in the last days there are going to be some difficult times. People will be self-centered and grasping; boastful, arrogant and rude; disobedient to their parents, ungrateful, irreligious; heartless and unappeasable; they will be slanderers, profligates, savages and enemies of everything that is good; they will be treacherous and reckless and demented by pride, preferring their own pleasure to God. They will keep the outward appearance of religion but will have rejected the inner power of it."[80]

11. Lord, we know also that as long as we live in this world, we are going to have to face

the work of the devil and his fellow demons. They are constantly trying to establish their counter-kingdom on earth, to which those described above belong. Inspire us to avoid membership in their realm at all costs. Rather, "Thy Kingdom come, on earth as it is in Heaven. And lead us not into temptation, but deliver us from evil."

12. Also, Lord, we pray for the conversion of all who are being used by the devil. Just as many of us were once spiritually dead in our sins and later came to life through Your saving power, so through our prayers and good works may those who are now in slavery to sin and to the evil one be released to enjoy Your friendship.

13. Most Sacred Heart of Jesus, St. Paul made another important point to St. Timothy. He said, "You are well aware, then, that anybody who tries to live in devotion to Christ

is certain to be attacked..."[81] This is so true, Lord, since the world loves darkness rather than light.[82] And inasmuch as wicked men attacked and crucified You, so shall Your true followers and friends be attacked, and some will even be put to death.

14. These are certainly not comforting words in themselves, Lord. Nobody likes to be attacked. Yet, assaults of this sort serve to demonstrate our loyalty to You. And what is more, to the degree that we suffer for Your sake, You will supply a corresponding consolation. "Indeed, as the sufferings of Christ overflow to us, so, through Christ, does our consolation overflow."[83]

15. Actually, Jesus, we should count it a privilege and joy to suffer and be opposed on Your account. As we have noted earlier, these are occasions for drawing even closer to You and for becoming increasingly holy. And the more we persevere under such attacks, we are correspondingly strengthened to be of greater service to You and our fellow men. Nor should we lose sight of the fact that even the consolations You give us while on earth for our loyalty to You under fire, are nothing compared to the joys that shall be ours in Heaven. The more we suffer for the sake of Your Name in this life, the happier we shall be in the next.

16. The last thing we would like to comment on today, Lord, is St. Paul's teaching about Scripture. He insists that since Scripture is divinely inspired, it can impart

"The wisdom that leads to salvation through faith in Christ Jesus."[84] Furthermore, he adds that Scripture, "can profitably be used for teaching, for refuting error, for guiding people's lives and teaching them to be holy."[85]

17. We are thankful, Jesus, that You have provided us with Holy Scripture as a guide to sanctity. May we read the Bible every day, and meditate on its teaching, in order to obtain the knowledge and wisdom which lead us to You and life everlasting. Amen.

Try to read these Scripture passages and meditations in a reflective manner every day. The Holy Spirit will reveal more insights to you each time you do so.

Please read and meditate on Chapter XIII, Paragraphs 1 to 17 of "Peaceful Seed Living," Volume II.

WEEK 2 DAY 6
Titus 1:1-16

Titus

THE LETTER FROM PAUL TO TITUS

Address

1 From Paul, servant of God, an apostle of Jesus Christ to bring those whom God has chosen to faith and to the knowledge of the 2 truth that leads to true religion; ·and to give them the hope of the eternal life that was promised so long ago by God. He does not 3 lie ·and so, at the appointed time, he revealed his decision, and, by the command of God our savior, I have been commissioned to pro-4 claim it. ·To Titus, true child of mine in the faith that we share, wishing you grace and peace from God the Father and from Christ Jesus our savior.

The appointment of elders

5 The reason I left you behind in Crete was for you to get everything organized there and appoint elders in every town, in the way that 6 I told you: ·that is, each of them must be a man of irreproachable character; he must not have been married more than once, and his children must be believers and not uncontrollable or liable to be charged with disorderly 7 conduct. ·Since, as president, he will be

God's representative, he must be irreproachable: never an arrogant or hot-tempered man, nor a heavy drinker or violent, nor out to
8 make money; ·but a man who is hospitable and a friend of all that is good; sensible,
9 moral, devout and self-controlled; ·and he must have a firm grasp of the unchanging message of the tradition, so that he can be counted on for both expounding the sound doctrine and refuting those who argue against it.

Opposing the false teachers

10 And in fact you have there a great many people who need to be disciplined, who talk nonsense and try to make others believe it, particularly among those of the Circumci-
11 sion. ·They have got to be silenced: men of this kind ruin whole families, by teaching things that they ought not to, and doing it
12 with the vile motive of making money. ·It was one of themselves, one of their own prophets, who said,*a* "Cretans were never anything but
13 liars, dangerous animals and lazy": ·and that is a true statement. So you will have to be severe in correcting them, and make them
14 sound in the faith ·so that they stop taking notice of Jewish myths and doing what they are told to do by people who are no longer interested in the truth.

15 To all who are pure themselves, everything is pure; but to those who have been corrupted and lack faith, nothing can be pure—the corruption is both in their minds and in their
16 consciences. ·They claim to have knowledge of God but the things they do are nothing but a denial of him; they are outrageously rebellious and quite incapable of doing good.

Week 2 Day 6
Four C's Reflections
on Titus 1:1-16

1. Today, Most Precious Savior, we paused to reflect on St. Paul's words to Titus, where he spoke of the hope for eternal life which You alone can provide.[86] We know, Lord, that prior to Your becoming man and prior to Your Resurrection and Ascension, eternal life in Your Father's Kingdom was an impossibility for mankind, since it was forfeited by the Fall of our first parents. Thus to have hope for eternal life during this period would have been fruitless. *(Be sure to read the introductory remarks about the Letter to Titus, beginning on p. 28 of this book.)*

2. The following passages from the Old Testament, Lord, clearly illustrate the hopelessness that existed prior to Your victory over the grave.

3. "Are your marvels meant for the dead,

154

can ghosts rise up to praise you? Who talks of your love in the grave, of your faithfulness in the place of perdition? Do they hear of your marvels in the dark, about your righteousness in the land of oblivion?"[87]

4. Also: "For my soul is all troubled, my life is on the brink of Sheol; I am numbered among those who go down to the Pit, a man bereft of strength: a man alone, down among the dead, among the slaughtered in the graves, among those you have forgotten, those deprived of your protecting hand."[88] With the revelation of the coming of the Messiah, however, hope arose in eternal life with God which the Messiah would make possible. *(Sheol or the Pit, refers to the shadowy domain of the dead.)*

5. Lord, we can never thank You enough for suffering, dying and rising to life again so that all men might enjoy life everlasting with You in Your heavenly Kingdom. We also thank You for giving us the supernatural virtue of hope (confidence), whereby we can have:

6. "A confident and unhesitating expectation, resting upon God's promises of eternal happiness to be obtained by the divinely appointed means. We hope for the enjoyment of God, Himself, and for all the aids necessary to obtain this. Also, we can hope for these benefits for others." *(Donald Atwater, ed., "A Catholic Dictionary," 1941, P. 250.)*

7. Furthermore, this theological virtue

enables us to have confidence in God's goodness and in the resurrection of the body at the end of time.

8. Besides Your Resurrection, Lord, Your Ascension into Heaven also serves to support our hope in a future life with the Holy Trinity and with the angels and saints. Since the time of the Ascension, You are now in Heaven not only as God, but also as man, the first human being dwelling there. Moreover, before you left this world, You told Your followers You were ascending into Heaven to prepare a place for us too.

9. "Do not let your hearts be troubled. Trust in God still, and trust in me. There are many rooms in my Father's house; if there were not, I should have told you. I am going now to prepare a place for you, and after I have gone and prepared you a place, I shall return to take you with me; so that where I am you

may be too. You know the way to the place where I am going."[89]

10. Lord, thank You for Your gift of hope (confidence) with which we can confidently expect the fulfillment of Your promises. May we never lose it.

11. Jesus, St. Paul instructed Titus that those who desire to be elders (priests) in Your Church, must have children who are well-behaved.[90] These words, which can be applied to all Christian parents, have a special significance today because improper behavior among young children and teenagers is so commonplace. This fact makes the conscientious parents' task of instilling correct beliefs and behavior in their children very difficult indeed. Also institutions, such as parish churches and church schools, are finding it increasingly difficult to bolster the parents' responsibility in these areas. *(In the period of the early Church, married men were allowed to be ordained priests.)*

12. It would seem that the only practical solution to this breakdown in behavior would be to have large numbers of parents, clergy, Religious, lay teachers and others work together to attack the underlying causes. The Apostolate for Family Consecration can be an effective guide and help in this area. As the Apostolate grows from neighborhood to neighborhood, children, parents and others will be strengthened and revitalized spiritually and morally, helping to strengthen and revitalize the rest of society.

13. Lastly, Lord, we were struck by St. Paul's famous statement on purity. "To all who are pure themselves, everything is pure; but to those who have been corrupted and lack faith, nothing can be pure — the corruption is both in their minds and in their consciences."[91] That is to say, those who keep their consciences pure or free from at least grave sin, lead a pure or holy life. But for those whose consciences are stained with grave sin, everything they do lacks sanctity, thus barring their way to Heaven. Those who have lost the virtue of faith are especially pitiable since they no longer have the supernatural light to lead them from their sins to Your friendship.

14. Most Sacred Heart of Jesus, You once said, "Happy the pure in heart: they shall see God."[92] Therefore, inspire us daily to repent of our sins, so that we will always be ready to behold God's presence in Heaven. Moreover, help us to love you more perfectly, so that we will have a greater capacity to enjoy the divine presence forever. Amen.

Try to read these Scripture passages and meditations in a reflective manner every day. The Holy Spirit will reveal more insights to you each time you do so.

Please read and meditate on Chapter XIII, Paragraphs 18 to 40 of "Peaceful Seed Living," Volume II.

WEEK 2 DAY 7
Titus 2:1-3:15

Some specific moral instruction

2 ¹It is for you, then, to preach the behavior ⁽ᶜ³⁾
²which goes with healthy doctrine. ·The
older men should be reserved, dignified, ⁽ᶜ²⁾
moderate, sound in faith and love and con- ⁽ᶜ¹⁾
³stancy. ·Similarly, the older women should ⁽ᶜ³⁾
⁽ᶜ⁴⁾
⁽ᶜ⁵⁾

behave as though they were religious, with ⁽ᶜ³⁾
no scandalmongering and no habitual wine- ⁽ᶜ²⁾
drinking—they are to be the teachers of the
⁴ right behavior ·and show the younger women
how they should love their husbands and love ⁽ᶜ³⁾
⁵ their children, ·how they are to be sensible ⁽ᶜ³⁾
and chaste, and how to work in their homes, ⁽ᶜ³⁾
and be gentle, and do as their husbands tell ⁽ᶜ²⁾
them, so that the message of God is never ⁽ᶜ³⁾
⁶ disgraced. ·In the same way, you have got to
persuade the younger men to be moderate
⁷ and in everything you do make yourself an ⁽ᶜ³⁾
example to them of working for good: when ⁽ᶜ³⁾
you are teaching, be an example to them in
⁸ your sincerity and earnestness ·and in keep- ⁽ᶜ³⁾
ing all that you say so wholesome that no- ⁽ᶜ³⁾
body can make objections to it; and then any
opponent will be at a loss, with no accusation ⁽ᶜ²⁾
⁹ to make against us. ·Tell the slaves that they
are to be obedient to their masters and always ⁽ᶜ³⁾
do what they want without any argument; ⁽ᶜ³⁾
¹⁰ and there must be no petty thieving—they ⁽ᶜ²⁾
must show complete honesty at all times, so ⁽ᶜ²⁾
that they are in every way a credit to the ⁽ᶜ³⁾
teaching of God our savior.

The basis of the Christian moral life

¹¹   You see, God's grace has been revealed,
and it has made salvation possible for the
¹² whole human race ·and taught us that what

we have to do is to give up everything that
does not lead to God, and all our worldly
ambitions; we must be self-restrained and live
good and religious lives here in this present
13 world, •while we are waiting in hope for the
blessing which will come with the Appearing
of the glory of our great God and savior
14 Christ Jesus.*a* •He sacrificed himself for us
in order to *set us free from all wickedness**b*
and *to purify a people so that it could be his
very own**c* and would have no ambition except
to do good.
15 Now this is what you are to say, whether
you are giving instruction or correcting errors; you can do so with full authority, and
no one is to question it.

General instruction for believers

3 Remind them that it is their duty to be
obedient to the officials and representatives of the government; to be ready to do
2 good at every opportunity; •not to go slandering other people or picking quarrels, but to
be courteous and always polite to all kinds of
3 people. •Remember, there was a time when
we too were ignorant, disobedient and misled
and enslaved by different passions and luxuries; we lived then in wickedness and ill-will,
hating each other and hateful ourselves.
4 But when the kindness and love of God

5 our savior for mankind were revealed, ·it was not because he was concerned with any righteous actions we might have done ourselves; it was for no reason except his own compassion that he saved us, by means of the cleansing water of rebirth and by renewing us with
6 the Holy Spirit ·which he has so generously poured over us through Jesus Christ our sav-
7 ior. ·He did this so that we should be justified by his grace, to become heirs looking for-
8 ward to inheriting eternal life. ·This is doctrine that you can rely on. (C1)

Personal advice to Titus

I want you to be quite uncompromising in (C3) teaching all this, so that those who now believe in God may keep their minds constantly (C1) occupied in doing good works. All this is (C4) good, and will do nothing but good to every-
9 body. ·But avoid pointless speculations, and (C2) those genealogies, and the quibbles and dis- (C2) putes about the Law—these are useless and (C2)
10 can do no good to anyone. ·If a man disputes what you teach, then after a first and a second (C2)
11 warning, have no more to do with him: ·you will know that any man of that sort has already lapsed and condemned himself as a sinner.

Practical recommendations, farewells and good wishes

12 As soon as I have sent Artemas or Tychicus to you, lose no time in joining me at Nicopolis, where I have decided to spend the
13 winter. ·See to all the traveling arrangements for Zenas the lawyer and Apollos, and make
14 sure they have everything they need. ·All our (C3) people are to learn to occupy themselves in doing good works for their practical needs as (C3) well, and not to be entirely unproductive.
15 All those who are with me send their greetings. Greetings to those who love us in the (C3) faith. Grace be with you all. (C3)

Week 2 Day 7
Four C's Reflections
on Titus 2:1-3:15

1. Most Merciful Savior, in today's meditation, St. Paul declared that Christian adults must exhibit certain types of correct behavior. Older men, for instance, "should be reserved, dignified, moderate, sound in faith and love and constancy."[93] St. Paul also wrote that older women are to show younger women, "how they should love their husbands and love their children, how they are to be sensible and chaste..."[94]

2. Basically, Lord, we see mentioned here all of Scripture's 4 C's, namely, confidence, conscience, seed-charity and constancy. May these be mirrored in our lives, since they are not only pleasing to You, but through them You are revealed to others.

3. Then, dear Jesus, St. Paul spoke of God's grace, or merciful kindness (benevolence), revealed to us (through You), which "made salvation possible for the whole human race."[95] Additionally, God taught

us, said St. Paul, that we are to be self-restrained, getting rid of everything that does not lead to Him, including our worldly ambitions. *(For a definition and discussion on the nature of grace, see the entry under "grace" on p. 236 of the "Modern Catholic Catechism.")*

4. Even in the best of circumstances, Lord, following the divine will in these matters is not easy when we first begin to dedicate our lives to God with confidence and seed-charity. But today it is especially hard, when almost everything around us encourages self-indulgence rather than self-restraint. We are being urged to involve ourselves in all sorts of things that do not lead to You, the Father and the Holy Spirit.

5. Newspapers, magazines, books, radio, and television are constantly pouring out non-Christian ideas and causes. These tend to weaken our faith in You and in the supernatural life of grace. We have in mind, for example, the abominable plague of

abortion. Until recently, very few people, living in what used to be known as the Christian West, defended abortion as an ethical practice approved by God. Yet, a small number of abortion advocates in positions of influence bombarded us continuously with the idea that abortion was not only right, but sometimes even necessary. Within a few years, the practice was upheld by the courts of one country after another. The fact a baby is killed in every act of abortion, and that millions are slaughtered in this way every year, was either overlooked or denied.

6. We also see, today, a parallel but more subtle "abortion" movement which encourages the easy breakup or "abortion" of families through divorce. In the earlier years of our century there were very few who condoned divorce, since most recognized it for the evil it really is. Yet today divorce is so widespread that nearly fifty per cent of all marriages now end in divorce in the United States alone. There are, of course, some just grounds for the separation of Christian spouses, such as instances when the physical and spiritual well-being of a family is threatened by an evil spouse. Nevertheless, the Church cannot grant permission to re-marry in even these cases.

7. Most Sacred Heart of Jesus, conveniently overlooked in the promotion of easy divorce is the fact that not only families are destroyed, but society as well. Also ignored is the children's natural right to have

both parents living in the home to rear them in charity and be models of marital love. When children do not experience the marital fidelity of their parents, is it any wonder that divorce breeds divorce?

8. When one or both parents seek a divorce in order to be "liberated" or "fulfilled" they are not taking into consideration the fundamental rights of their children.

9. Lord, help parents to stay close to Your Sacred Heart. May they, through Your graces and through fervent prayer and the sacraments, be firmly committed to their marriage vows. May they resist the ever-present voices encouraging self-indulgence and the neglect of grave responsibilities. And may their children's rights and needs always be foremost in their hearts and minds. *(See "The Catholic Catechism," pp. 364-367, for information on marital fidelity, and pp. 356-362 for a discussion on martial indissolubility.)*

10. Jesus, in chapter three of Titus, St. Paul says Christians are to be obedient to government officials.[96]

11. St. Peter made the same point when he wrote:

12. "For the sake of the Lord, accept the authority of every social institution: the emperor, as the supreme authority, and the governors as commissioned by him to punish criminals and praise good citizenship. God wants you to be good citizens..."[97]

13. We Christians, Lord, are not above the civil or secular law, as long as it conforms to Your will. Moreover, these passages support the principle that Christians are to involve themselves in secular fields in order to improve society, thus bringing it closer to You.

14. We must, however, refrain from conforming to those laws or practices which do not reflect Your will. In such instances we are bound to follow St. Peter's cry that "Obedience to God comes before obedience to men."[98]

15. Divine Savior, St. Paul once more emphasized the fact that we sinners in no way merited our redemption.

16. "But when the kindness and love of God our savior for mankind were revealed, it was not because he was concerned with any righteous actions we might have done ourselves; it was for no reason except his own

compassion that he saved us . . ."[99]

17. Thus, Lord, we again see clearly that it was because we were helpless to save ourselves that You, the Father and the Holy Spirit, planned to bring us into Your eternal presence through Your sacrifice on the Cross and through the sacraments of the Church, beginning with Baptism. But, as we also observed in an earlier meditation, this does not mean that once we begin to share in Your victory over sin and death through the waters of Baptism, we have no role to play in maintaining our salvation and in meriting increases in sanctity. Indeed, we do. But even so, all our meritorious acts are begun, continued and completed by Your grace. We simply cooperate with it by the free exercise of our wills.

18. Most Merciful Messiah, we can never thank You enough for all You have done and are continuing to do for us so we can obtain eternal happiness. And we must express our gratitude through leading holy lives of self-sacrifice for others through our prayers and good works, and through devotion to You, the Father and the Holy Spirit, especially in the most holy Sacrifice of the Mass. Lord, we also ask Your unending assistance in these endeavors. Amen.

Try to read these Scripture passages and meditations in a reflective manner every day. The Holy Spirit will reveal more insights to you each time you do so.

Please read and meditate on Chapter XIV, Paragraphs 1 to 9 and Chapter XV, Paragraphs 1 to 2 of "Peaceful Seed Living," Volume II.

WEEK 3 DAY 1
Philemon 1-25

Philemon

THE LETTER FROM PAUL TO PHILEMON

Address

1 From Paul, a prisoner of Christ Jesus and from our brother Timothy; to our dear fellow
2 worker Philemon, ·our sister Apphia, our fellow soldier Archippus and the church that
3 meets in your house; ·wishing you the grace and the peace of God our Father and the Lord Jesus Christ.

Thanksgiving and prayer

4 I always mention you in my prayers and
5 thank God for you, ·because I hear of the

love and the faith which you have for the (C3)
6 Lord Jesus and for all the saints. •I pray that (C1)
this faith will give rise to a sense of fellowship (C1)
that will show you all the good things that we
7 are able to do for Christ. •I am so delighted, (C3)

and comforted, to know of your love; they tell (C3)
me, brother, how you have put new heart into (C3)
the saints.

The request about Onesimus

8 Now, although in Christ I can have no
diffidence about telling you to do whatever
9 is your duty, •I am appealing to your love (C3)
instead, reminding you that this is Paul writing, an old man now and, what is more, still
10 a prisoner of Christ Jesus. •I am appealing
to you for a child of mine, whose father I
became while wearing these chains: I mean
11 Onesimus. •He was of no use to you before,
but he will be useful[a] to you now, as he has
12 been to me. •I am sending him back to you,
and with him—I could say—a part of my own
13 self. •I should have liked to keep him with me;
he could have been a substitute for you, to
help me while I am in the chains that the
14 Good News has brought me. •However, I did
not want to do anything without your con-
sent; it would have been forcing your act of (C3)
15 kindness, which should be spontaneous. •I
know you have been deprived of Onesimus
for a time, but it was only so that you could
16 have him back for ever, •not as a slave any

more, but something much better than a
slave, a dear brother; especially dear to me,
but how much more to you, as a blood-
17 brother as well as a brother in the Lord. •So if
all that we have in common means anything to
18 you, welcome him as you would me; •but if he (C3)
has wronged you in any way or owes you any- (C2)
19 thing, then let me pay for it. •I am writing (C3)
this in my own handwriting: I, Paul, shall pay
it back—I will not add any mention of your (C3)

169

20 own debt to me, which is yourself. ·Well then,
brother, I am counting on you, in the Lord; put
21 new heart into me, in Christ. ·I am writing
with complete confidence in your compliance, (C3)
sure that you will do even more than I ask. (C3)

A personal request. Good wishes

22 There is another thing: will you get a place
ready for me to stay in? I am hoping through
your prayers to be restored to you. (C3
23 Epaphras, a prisoner with me in Christ
24 Jesus, sends his greetings; ·so do my col- (C3)
leagues Mark, Aristarchus, Demas and Luke.
25 May the grace of our Lord Jesus Christ be (C3)
with your spirit.

Week 3 Day 1
Four C's Reflections
on Philemon 1-25

1. Most Sacred Heart of Jesus, in his Letter to Philemon St. Paul writes that he always mentioned Philemon in his prayers.[100] He was also fulfilling Your commandment to love one another.[102] (Be sure to read the introductory remarks about the Letter to Philemon on p. 29 of this book.)

2. Yes, Lord, when we pray for the well-being of others we are exercising charity. And since You taught us we are to love even our enemies and to pray for those who persecute us, we must pray for them as well.[103]

3. Jesus, it may well be You have determined from all eternity that it will be our prayers on behalf of our enemies, for example, which will be the means of drawing them closer to You. Moreover, our prayers may well be Your providential instruments for making our enemies no longer our adversaries, but our friends.

4. Others for whom we should pray, Lord, are members of our families, the Poor Souls in Purgatory, the sick, our friends, relatives, bishops, clergy, Religious, teachers, and governmental leaders, as well as those who have no one else (as far as we know) to pray for them.

5. Most Merciful Savior, may our prayers for one another, especially those offered up at

Mass, strengthen the ties that bind us spiritually, thus contributing to the building up of Your Mystical Body the Church.

6. We know too, Lord, that our prayers for others, recited in charity, merit graces for ourselves and are means of penance. *(See "The Catholic Catechism," pp. 558-559 for information on prayer as a means of penance.)*

7. Jesus, we should also remember the effectiveness of praying the Rosary for others, and the benefits we can obtain for others through the intercessory power of Your Blessed Mother, St. Joseph and all the angels and saints.

8. Jesus, in his Letter to Philemon, St. Paul reveals a profound concern for Philemon's runaway slave, Onesimus. We have particularly in mind St. Paul's request that, upon being returned to his master, Onesimus should no longer be treated as a slave but as a

blood brother and a brother in Christ. We see displayed here a love for others that transcends class barriers. It is a selfless love that can transform its givers into saints. It is, of course, seed-charity.

9. Self-sacrificing acts like St. Paul's are very pleasing to You, Lord. Moreover, opportunities to perform them for others are endless.

10. There are, for instance, the sick and dying, the lonely and depressed, the poor, those in prison and those suffering for their religious and political beliefs. These, and others, who are often living near us, we could visit and comfort with very little effort.

11. Many of us, Lord, spend several hours a day devoted to our own comfort, such as watching television and reading. Is it too much, then, for us to spend some time comforting the suffering?

12. Most importantly, we should be concerned with the needs of our own families. Some of us have not been paying enough attention to our spouses and children. As a matter of fact, some of us have been so busy looking after the needs of others, what we may have rarely taken time to be with those of our own household. Jesus, help us always to be concerned with the needs of others, but especially with the needs of our families.

13. Lord, in the case of Onesimus, the slave, not only did St. Paul intercede on

Onesimus' behalf to his master Philemon, St. Paul also generously offered to pay any debt the slave might have incurred. This is especially remarkable in light of the fact that St. Paul was not a wealthy man.

14. But it is in keeping with what we know of his generous spirit. We need recall only the fact that he frequently supported himself by working with his own hands, rather than become a burden on those from whom he could justly expect financial remuneration.

15. Lord, generosity is a mark of sanctity. Help us to be more generous in meeting the needs of others, whether friends or foes, by making ourselves more available. Amen.

Try to read these Scripture passages and meditations in a reflective manner every day. The Holy Spirit will reveal more insights to you each time you do so.

Please refer to Chapter XVI, Paragraphs 1-9; XVII, Paragraphs 1 to 2; and XVIII, Paragraphs 1-4 of our "Peaceful Seed Living," Volume II.

WEEK 3 DAY 2
Hebrews 1:1-3:19

THE LETTER TO THE

Hebrews

A Letter Addressed
to a Jewish-Christian Community

PROLOGUE

The greatness of the incarnate Son of God

¹ At various times in the past and in various different ways, God spoke to our ances- ² tors through the prophets; but ·in our own time, the last days, he has spoken to us through his Son, the Son that he has appointed to inherit everything and through ³ whom he made everything there is. ·He is the radiant light of God's glory and the perfect copy of his nature, sustaining the universe by his powerful command; and now that he has destroyed the defilement of sin, he has gone (C2) to take his place in heaven at the right hand ⁴ of divine Majesty. ·So he is now as far above

the angels as the title which he has inherited is higher than their own name.

I. THE SON IS GREATER THAN THE ANGELS

Proof from the scriptures

⁵ God has never said to any angel: *You are my Son, today I have become your father;*[a] or: *I will be a father to him and he a son to*

6 *me.ᵇ* •Again, when he brings the Firstborn
into the world, he says: *Let all the angels of*
7 *God worship him.ᶜ* •About the angels, he
says: *He makes his angels winds and his serv-*
8 *ants flames of fire,ᵈ* •but to his Son he says:
God, your throne shall last for ever and ever;
and: *his royal sceptre is the sceptre of virtue;*
9 *virtue you love as much as you hate wicked-*
ness. This is why God, your God, has
anointed you with the oil of gladness, above
10 *all your rivals.ᵉ* •And again: *It is you, Lord,*
who laid earth's foundations in the beginning,

11 *the heavens are the work of your hands;* •*all*
will vanish, though you remain, all wear out
12 *like a garment;* •*you will roll them up like a*
cloak, and like a garment *they will be*
changed. But yourself, you never change and
13 *your years are unending.ᶠ* •God has never
said to any angel: *Sit at my right hand and*
I will make your enemies a footstool for
14 *you.ᵍ* •The truth is they are all spirits whose
work is service, sent to help those who will (C3)
be the heirs of salvation.

An exhortation

1 2 We ought, then, to turn our minds more
attentively than before to what we have (C1)
been taught, so that we do not drift away. (C2)
2 If a promise that was made through angelsᵃ

proved to be so true that every infringement
and disobedience brought its own proper (C2)
3 punishment, ·then we shall certainly not go
unpunished if we neglect this salvation that (C2)
is promised to us. The promise was first announced by the Lord himself, and is guaran-
4 teed to us by those who heard him; ·God (C1)
himself confirmed their witness with signs
and marvels and miracles of all kinds, and by
freely giving the gifts of the Holy Spirit.

Redemption brought by Christ, not by angels

5 He did not appoint angels to be rulers of
the world to come, and that world is what we
6 are talking about. ·Somewhere there is a passage that shows us this. It runs: *What is man
that you should spare a thought for him, the
son of man that you should care for him?*
7 *For a short while you made him lower than
the angels; you crowned him with glory and*
8 *splendor.* ·*You have put him in command of
everything.*[b] Well then, if he has *put him in
command of everything,* he has left nothing
which is not under his command. At present, it is true, we are not able to see that
everything has been put under his command,
9 but we do see in Jesus one who was *for
a short while made lower than the angels* and
is now *crowned with glory and splendor* because he submitted to death; by God's
grace he had to experience death for all mankind.
10 As it was his purpose to bring a great many
of his sons into glory, it was appropriate that

God, for whom everything exists and through
whom everything exists, should make perfect, through suffering, the leader who would
11 take them to their salvation. ·For the one who
sanctifies, and the ones who are sanctified, (C2)
are of the same stock; that is why he openly
12 calls them *brothers* ·in the text: *I shall an-
nounce your name to my brothers, praise you*

13 *in full assembly;*[c] or the text: •*In him I hope;* or the text: *Here I am with the children whom God has given me.*[d]

14 Since all the *children* share the same blood and flesh, he too shared equally in it, so that by his death he could take away all the power
15 of the devil, who had power over death, •and set free all those who had been held in slavery (C2)
16 all their lives by the fear of death. •For it was not the angels that he took to himself; he took
17 to himself *descent from Abraham.*[e] •It was essential that he should in this way become completely like his brothers so that he could be a compassionate and trustworthy high priest of God's religion, able to atone for
18 human sins. •That is, because he has himself been through temptation he is able to help others who are tempted.

II. JESUS THE FAITHFUL AND MERCIFUL HIGH PRIEST

Christ higher than Moses

1 **3** That is why all you who are holy brothers (C2) and have had the same heavenly call

should turn your minds to Jesus, the apostle
and the high priest of our religion. •He was
faithful to the one who appointed him, just
like *Moses,* who stayed faithful *in all his
house;* •but he has been found to deserve a
greater glory than Moses. It is the difference
between the honor given to the man that built
the house and to the house itself. •Every
house is built by someone, of course; but
God built everything that exists. •It is true
that Moses was *faithful in the house* of God,
as a servant, acting as witness to the things
which were to be divulged later; •but Christ
was faithful as a son, and as the master in the
house. And we are his house, as long as we
cling to our hope with the confidence that we
glory in.

How to reach God's land of rest

7 The Holy Spirit says: *If only you would
8 listen to him today;* •*do not harden your
hearts, as happened in the Rebellion, on the
9 Day of Temptation in the wilderness,* •*when
your ancestors challenged me and tested me,
10 though they had seen what I could do* •*for
forty years. That was why I was angry with
that generation and said: How unreliable
these people who refuse to grasp my ways!
11 And so, in anger, I swore that not one would
12 reach the place of rest I had for them.*ᵃ •Take
care, brothers, that there is not in any one of
your community a wicked mind, so unbelieving as to turn away from the living God.
13 Every day, as long as this "today" lasts, keep
encouraging one another so that none of you
14 is *hardened* by the lure of sin, •because we
shall remain co-heirs with Christ only if we
keep a grasp on our first confidence right to
15 the end. •In this saying: *If only you would
listen to him today; do not harden your hearts,*

16 *as happened in the Rebellion,* •those who *re-
belled* after they had *listened* were all the

people who were brought out of Egypt by
17 Moses. •And those who made God *angry for forty years* were the ones who sinned and (C2) whose *dead bodies were left lying in the wil-*
18 *derness.*[b] •Those that he *swore would never reach the place of rest he had for them* were
19 those who had been disobedient. •We see, (C2) then, that it was because they were unfaithful (C2) that they were not able to reach it.

Week 3 Day 2
Four C's Reflections
on Hebrews 1:1-3:19

1. Most Sacred Heart of Jesus, we have begun to meditate on the Letter to the Hebrews, the theme of which is the superiority of the New (Christian) Covenant over the Old Covenant made with the Hebrew people. Already, we have received many spiritual insights. *(Be sure to read the introductory remarks about the letter to the Hebrews, beginning on p. 30 of this book.)*

2. In the very beginning of the letter, our attention was drawn to the statement that God the Father created and sustains the entire universe through You, His eternal Son.[104] Your motive for creating and sustaining the universe was simply Your free and unselfish love. This is true, since You, the Father and the Holy Spirit contain within Yourselves, all perfections and all happiness, and therefore have no need of creatures to fulfill or satisfy You in any way. *(See "The Catholic Catechism," pp. 63-67, 72-83, for discussions on the Trinity and on creation.)*

3. Lord, we can never thank You enough for creating the universe. We are especially grateful for our own creation and the fact that, from all eternity, You desired us to be elevated above the level of our human nature to share in Your own divinity.

4. We also thank You for Your on-going love in spite of our sins. You loved us so much You became one of us, yet without sin, so that through Your sacrifice on the Cross, we might become sons of God for ever.

5. Jesus, there can be no greater love than Yours for us poor sinners. Lord, grant that we may always respond to this love with grateful hearts through the use of Your supernatural gift of seed-charity. And may we, in turn, allow this gift to shine through our lives for the benefit of others, especially for those closest to us.

6. Now, Lord, we would like to speak a few moments about angels who are so frequently mentioned in today's meditation. We have reference particularly to the following words: "The truth is they are all spirits whose work is service, sent to help those who will be heirs of salvation."[105] *(For a presentation on angels, read "The Catholic Catechism," pp. 83-90.)*

7. Today, as You are well aware, Lord, angels are seldom mentioned in our part of the world. Yet they play a vital role in our salvation. Although they, like us, are intelligent creatures with free wills, they are unlike us in the fact they are pure spirits. That is, they have no material bodies subject to death and corruption. Nor are they in need of a savior, since they never fell from Your friendship, and they are now citizens of Your heavenly Kingdom. *(There are also fallen angels, commonly called demons, who fell from grace and were condemned to perdition.)*

8. Like ourselves, the angels were created to serve You and others. In particular, as we just noted, they are "sent to help those who will be heirs of salvation." Furthermore, Your Catholic Church holds that every one of the

faithful has his or her guardian angel, who is sent to protect and guide us on our way to salvation. And we are encouraged to invoke their aid, just as we are encouraged to seek the help of the saints.

9. Lord Jesus, we thank You for the existence of our guardian angels who serve You by serving us. May we never fail to invoke their help.

10. Most Merciful Savior, we were reminded in today's meditation of the importance of dedicating our lives to God daily, so the saving grace You merited for us on the Cross can work in us. Otherwise, "We shall certainly not go unpunished..."(106) Lord, we must find a time and a place to offer ourselves to the Triune God each day. Ideally, it should be within the context of the Holy Sacrifice of the Mass where we and our prayers, inspired by the Holy Spirit, are joined to Your perfect and eternal sacrifice. And through Your sacrifice, we are accepted by the Father. But if this is not possible, any

time and place which are convenient and suitable will do, although a church or chapel would be preferable locations.

11. Nor should we hold back any part of our soul, either from Yourself, the Father, or the Holy Spirit since You wish to sanctify it in its entirety as St. Teresa of Avila taught.

12. "The important thing is that we should be completely determined to give it to Him for His own and should empty it so that He may take out and put in just what He wishes, as He would with something of His own. His Majesty is right in requiring this; let us not deny it to Him. Since He refuses to force our wills, He takes what we give Him but does not give Himself fully until He sees that we are giving ourselves fully to Him. This is certain, and since it is so important I remind you of it often. Nor does He operate within the soul as He does when it is completely His and nothing is withheld from Him." *("The Way of Perfection," Ch. 25, section 12.)*

13. Jesus, You greatly comfort the souls of those who give themselves unreservedly to You. Grant that we may always clearly see the futility of witholding from You even the smallest part of our lives. Indeed, Lord, full happiness will never be ours until we are completely Yours.

14. Most Sacred Heart of Jesus, in our reading for today, our attention was drawn to the following passage:

15. "Take care, brothers, that there is not in

any one of your community a wicked mind, so unbelieving as to turn away from the living God. Every day, as long as this 'today' lasts, keep encouraging one another so that none of you is hardened by the lure of sin, because we shall remain co-heirs with Christ only if we keep a grasp on our first confidence right to the end."[107]

16. These words, Lord, brought to mind the awesome responsibility parents have for the spiritual well-being of their children. Parents are obliged to do all in their power to protect their offspring from unbelief and all other forms of sin.

17. We have, in an earlier meditation, already spoken about the importance of providing children with an education that is completely Catholic. This will do much to help them not to waver in their faith and confidence in You, Lord. On the other hand, education in itself is not sufficient to prevent sin. Most children, as do many adults, have weak wills, and in our culture temptations to sin abound. Therefore, parents must do all they can to reduce the occasions for sin. They must, for example, know where their children are at all times, what they are doing, and whom they are with.

18. Today, Lord, we cannot even assume that Catholic schools are havens from occasions of sin. We have in mind, particularly, drug abuse and ideas contrary to Catholic morality. Parents should no longer take it for granted that school administrators

and teachers can handle problems like these without the parents' active involvement and cooperation.

19. Children must also be taught to pray privately, and with their families as well. Additionally, parents should help their children worship well at Mass and at other public ceremonies of the Church.

20. Jesus, Mary and Joseph, help parents to become increasingly aware of the many dangers their children are exposed to daily. And may they take seriously their responsibilities for being the primary guardians of their children's spiritual welfare, remembering You will severely judge those who fail to do so.[108] Amen.

Try to read these Scripture passages and meditations in a reflective manner every day. The Holy Spirit will reveal more insights to you each time you do so.

Please refer to Chapter XIX, Paragraphs 1 to 21 of "Peaceful Seed Living," Volume II.

WEEK 3 DAY 3
Hebrews 4:1-5:14

4 ¹ Be careful, then: the promise of *reaching the place of rest he had for them* still holds good, and none of you must think that he has ² come too late for it. ·We received the Good News exactly as they did; but hearing the message did them no good because they did (C2) ³ not share the faith of those who listened. ·We, (C4) however, who have faith, shall reach a place (C1) of rest, as in the text: *And so, in anger, I swore that not one would reach the place of rest I had for them.* God's work was undoubtedly all finished at the beginning of the world; ⁴ as one text says, referring to the seventh day: *After all his work God rested on the seventh* ⁵ *day.*ᵃ ·The text we are considering says: *They shall not reach the place of rest I had for* ⁶ *them.* ·It is established, then, that there would be some people who would reach it, and since those who first heard the Good News failed to reach it through their disobedience, (C2) ⁷ God fixed another day when, much later, he said "today" through David in the text already quoted: *If only you would listen to him* (C1) ⁸ *today; do not harden your hearts.* ·If Joshua (C2) had led them into this place of rest, God would not later on have spoken so much of ⁹ another day. ·There must still be, therefore, a place of rest reserved for God's people, the ¹⁰ seventh-day rest, ·since to *reach the place of rest* is to *rest after your work,* as God did after ¹¹ his. ·We must therefore do everything we can (C3) to *reach this place of rest,* or some of you (C4) might copy this example of disobedience and (C2) be lost.

The word of God and Christ the priest

12 The word of God is something alive and

active: it cuts like any double-edged sword but more finely: it can slip through the place where the soul is divided from the spirit, or joints from the marrow; it can judge the se-
13 cret emotions and thoughts. •No created thing can hide from him; everything is uncovered and open to the eyes of the one to whom we must give account of ourselves.

14 Since in Jesus, the Son of God, we have the supreme high priest who has gone through to the highest heaven, we must never let go of the faith that we have professed. (C1)
15 For it is not as if we had a high priest who was incapable of feeling our weaknesses with us; but we have one who has been tempted in every way that we are, though he is without
16 sin. •Let us be confident, then, in approaching the throne of grace, that we shall have mercy from him and find grace when we are in need of help. (C1) (C2)

Jesus the compassionate high priest

1 5 Every high priest has been taken out of mankind and is appointed to act for men in their relations with God, to offer gifts and
2 sacrifices for sins; and so •he can sympathize with those who are ignorant or uncertain be- (C2) (C3)

cause he too lives in the limitations of weakness. ·That is why he has to make sin offerings for himself as well as for the people. (C3)
4 No one takes this honor on himself, but each
5 one is called by God, as Aaron was. ·Nor did Christ give himself the glory of becoming high priest, but he had it from the one who said to him: *You are my son, today I have
6 become your father,*[a] ·and in another text: *You are a priest of the order of Melchizedek, and
7 for ever.*[b] ·During his life on earth, he offered up prayer and entreaty, aloud and in silent tears, to the one who had the power to save him out of death, and he submitted so humbly
8 that his prayer was heard. ·Although he was Son, he learned to obey through suffering;
9 but having been made perfect, he became for all who obey him the source of eternal salva-
10 tion ·and was acclaimed by God with the title of high priest *of the order of Melchizedek.*

III. THE AUTHENTIC PRIESTHOOD OF JESUS CHRIST

Christian life and theology

11 On this subject we have many things to

say, and they are difficult to explain because you have grown so slow at understanding. (C2)
12 Really, when you should by this time have become masters, you need someone to teach you all over again the elementary principles of interpreting God's oracles; you have gone back to needing milk, and not solid
13 food. ·Truly, anyone who is still living on milk cannot digest the doctrine of righteous-
14 ness because he is still a baby. ·Solid food is for mature men with minds trained by practice to distinguish between good and bad.

Week 3 Day 3
Four C's Reflections
on Hebrews 4:1-5:14

1. Today's meditation, Most Holy Jesus, begins with a note of hope. Referring to Heaven as God's place of rest, which He prepared for all mankind, the author of Hebrews tells us that we must never believe it is too late to qualify for admission.[109] Consequently, we must not lose the hope that salvation for us is always possible.

2. Without hope, Lord, we cannot gain entrance into Heaven. Without hope, we would fall into the sin of despair and no longer trust in You, the Source of our salvation and eternal happiness. Thus, even if we commit a mortal sin and are deprived of Your friendship, we should not despair, since as long as we are in this world, we can sincerely and sorrowfully confess our sins, receive priestly absolution and restoration to Your friendship.

3. On the other hand, Lord, we must avoid the sin of presumption, which is also opposed to the supernatural virtue of hope. Presumption, as You have taught us through Your Church, is the sin of thinking we can enter Heaven solely by our own efforts, or arrogantly claiming we are not in a state of mortal sin when in fact we are, or supposing we will enter Heaven even if we die in the state of mortal sin.

4. As necessary as the supernatural virtues of faith and hope are for our salvation, Jesus, we must also have seed-charity, since faith and hope by themselves are not sufficient to merit us eternal life. By the exercise of seed-charity, we will always have faith and hope as well, and most importantly, we will remain in Your friendship and become increasingly holy.

5. Jesus, through Your mercy and protection, may we never lose our supernatural gifts of faith, hope and charity.

6. Lord, today's Scripture reading contains a well-known statement concerning You as our merciful and gracious High Priest.

7. "Since in Jesus, the Son of God, we have the supreme high priest who has gone through to the highest heaven, we must never let go of the faith that we have professed. For it is not as if we had a high priest who was incapable of feeling our weaknesses with us; but we have one who has been tempted in every way that we are, though he is without sin. Let us be confident, then, in approaching the throne of grace, that we shall have mercy from him and find grace when we are in the need of help."[110]

8. Our sinful condition, Lord, due initially to the Fall, excluded us from Your divine friendship in Heaven. Moreover, there was nothing we fallen creatures could do to merit the restoration of Your friendship and our participation in the supernatural life of grace. Even if we humans had never sinned, we could never have merited, in the first instance, the supernatural gifts which make us become God's friends and His adopted children. *(For a detailed presentation of the supernatural life of grace read pp. 177-185 of "The Catholic Catechism.")*

9. But when we did in fact fall from grace, You, Who are divine, in Your great charity and mercy humbled Yourself and became one of us. Then, acting as the perfect High Priest and Mediator between us and the Father, you restored to us the supernatural

life and access to Heaven. Also, while on earth as our supreme High Priest, You experienced temptation and all our natural human limitations, yet without sinning.

10. Thus, Lord, You are One Who, having experienced our condition, fully understands us. And when we experience Your friendship, we have a true Friend Who suffered for us and felt the full impact of the forces of evil which constantly wage war against mankind.

11. No greater Friend can we have than You Who laid down Your life for us, and Who sympathizes with our weaknesses.[111] Therefore, Lord, may we never be afraid to approach You humbly, lovingly and with confidence, knowing that when we do, You will never let us down in our moments of need.

12. Thank You, Jesus, so very much for Your sacrificial love and tender mercy towards us. May we show our appreciation by worshipping You, especially at Mass, and by sharing You with others through our words and in our deeds.

13. Most Sacred Heart of Jesus, the following four verses in our meditation speak eloquently of Your love for us and for Your heavenly Father.

14. "During this life on earth, he offered up prayer and entreaty, aloud and in silent tears, to the one who had the power to save him out of death, and he submitted so humbly that his prayer was heard. Although he was Son, he

learned to obey through suffering; but having been made perfect, he became for all who obey him the source of eternal salvation and he was acclaimed by God with the title of high priest . . ."[112]

15. Lord, these words should humble us. You chose to become one of us out of pure love and to suffer as You did for our sake in order to show us how much we mean to you. Forgive us for failing to appreciate sufficiently what You have done for us. And may we learn increasingly to imitate Your humble example of obedience to the Father and Your love for Your brothers in the flesh.

16. Jesus, today's Scripture reading also refers to those Christians who were not maturing as they should in the Faith. Consequently, they had to be treated as spiritual infants.[113]

17. Unfortunately, many of us are still babes in the Faith. As a result, we have not made much progress on the road to sanctity. Too often we have been content with doing as little as possible to remain in Your friendship. Yet, we should keep in mind the examples of the saints who were once themselves ordinary people, before their perseverance in Christian living gained them spiritual maturity.

18. They exerted themselves in leading lives as Your devoted disciples and they were consequently rewarded with Your intimacy and an abundance of Your grace. Furthermore, as they became more advanced in the spiritual life, they were more capable of helping others attain salvation and sanctity.

19. Lord, always inspire us to overcome spiritual laziness which retards our spiritual growth and prevents others, who might otherwise be attracted to deeper devotion and holiness, from seeing You clearly in us. Amen.

Try to read these Scripture passages and meditations in a reflective manner every day. The Holy Spirit will reveal more insights to you each time you do so.

Please refer to the page immediately preceding Chapter XX, Paragraphs 1-2; Chapter XXI, Paragraphs 1-5; and Chapter XXII, Paragraphs 1-5 of our "Peaceful Seed Living," Volume II.

WEEK 3 DAY 4
Hebrews 6:1-8:13

The author explains his intention

6 ¹Let us leave behind us then all the elementary teaching about Christ and concentrate on its completion, without going over the fundamental doctrines again: the turning away from dead actions and toward faith in ²God; ·the teaching about the resurrection of ³the dead and eternal judgment. ·This, God willing, is what we propose to do. (C2) (C1)

⁴ As for those people who were once brought into the light, and tasted the gift from heaven, and received a share of the Holy ⁵Spirit, ·and appreciated the good message of God and the powers of the world to come ⁶and yet in spite of this have fallen away—it is impossible for them to be renewed a second time. They cannot be repentant if they have willfully crucified the Son of God and ⁷openly mocked him ·A field that has been well watered by frequent rain, and gives the crops that are wanted by the owners who ⁸grew them, is given God's blessing; ·but one (C1) (C3) (C2)

that grows brambles and thistles is abandoned, and practically cursed. It will end by being burned.

Words of hope and encouragement

9 But you, my dear people—in spite of what we have just said, we are sure you are in a
10 better state and on the way to salvation. ·God would not be so unjust as to forget all you have done, the love that you have for his name or the services you have done, and are
11 still doing, for the saints.*a* ·Our one desire is that every one of you should go on showing the same earnestness to the end, to the per-
12 fect fulfillment of our hopes, ·never growing careless, but imitating those who have the faith and the perseverance to inherit the promises.
13 When God made the promise to Abraham, he *swore by his own self,* since it was impossi-
14 ble for him to swear by anyone greater: ·*I will shower blessings on you and give you many*
15 *descendants.b* ·Because of that, Abraham per-
16 severed and saw the promise fulfilled. ·Men, of course, swear an oath by something greater than themselves, and between men, confirmation by an oath puts an end to all

17 dispute. ·In the same way, when God wanted to make the heirs to the promise thoroughly realize that his purpose was unalterable, he
18 conveyed this by an oath; ·so that there would be two unalterable things in which it was impossible for God to be lying, and so that we, now we have found safety, should have a strong encouragement to take a firm grip (C4)
19 on the hope that is held out to us. ·Here we (C1) have an anchor for our soul, as sure as it is (C2) firm, and reaching right *through beyond the* (C4)
20 *veil*[c] ·where Jesus has entered before us and

on our behalf, to become a high *priest of the order of Melchizedek, and for ever.*

A. CHRIST'S PRIESTHOOD HIGHER THAN LEVITICAL PRIESTHOOD

Melchizedek[a]

1 **7** You remember that *Melchizedek, king of Salem, a priest of God Most High, went to meet Abraham who was on his way back after defeating the kings, and blessed him;*
2 and also that it was to him that Abraham gave *a tenth of all that he had.* By the interpretation of his name, he is, first, "king of righteousness" and also *king of Salem,* that is,
3 "king of peace"; ·he has no father, mother or ancestry, and his life has no beginning or ending; he is like the Son of God. He remains a priest for ever.

Melchizedek accepted tithes from Abraham

4 Now think how great this man must have been, if the patriarch *Abraham paid him a*
5 *tenth of the treasure he had captured.*[b] ·We know that any of the descendants of Levi who are admitted to the priesthood are obliged by the Law to take tithes from the people, and this is taking them from their own brothers although they too are descended from Abra-

6 ham. ·But this man, who was not of the same descent, took his tenth from Abraham, and he gave his blessing to the holder of the 7 promises. ·Now it is indisputable that a blessing is given by a superior to an inferior. 8 Further, in the one case it is ordinary mortal men who receive the tithes, and in the other, someone who is declared to be still alive. 9 It could be said that Levi himself, who receives tithes, actually paid them, in the per- 10 son of Abraham, ·because he was still in the loins of his ancestor when *Melchizedek came to meet him.*

From levitical priesthood to the priesthood of Melchizedek

11 Now if perfection had been reached through the levitical priesthood because the Law given to the nation rests on it, why was it still necessary for a new priesthood to arise, one *of the same order as Melchizedek*[c] not counted as being "of the same order as" 12 Aaron? ·But any change in the priesthood must mean a change in the Law as well.
13 So our Lord, of whom these things were said, belonged to a different tribe, the members of which have never done service at the 14 altar; ·everyone knows he came from Judah, a tribe which Moses did not even mention when dealing with priests.

The abrogation of the old Law

15 This[d] becomes even more clearly evident when there appears a second Melchizedek, 16 who is a priest ·not by virtue of a law about physical descent, but by the power of an inde- 17 structible life. ·For it was about him that the prophecy was made: *You are a priest of the or-* 18 *der of Melchizedek, and for ever.* ·The earlier commandment is thus abolished, because it 19 was neither effective nor useful, ·since the Law could not make anyone perfect; but now this commandment is replaced by something

better—the hope that brings us nearer to God. (C1)

Christ's priesthood is unchanging

20 What is more, this was not done without the taking of an oath. The others, indeed,
21 were made priests without any oath; ·but he with an oath sworn by the one who declared to him: *The Lord has sworn an oath which he will never retract: you are a priest, and for
22 ever.*[e] ·And it follows that it is a greater covenant for which Jesus has become our guaran-
23 tee. ·Then there used to be a great number of those other priests, because death put an
24 end to each one of them; ·but this one, because he remains *for ever,* can never lose his
25 priesthood. ·It follows, then, that his power to save is utterly certain, since he is living for ever to intercede for all who come to God through him.

The perfection of the heavenly high priest

26 To suit us, the ideal high priest would have to be holy, innocent and uncontaminated, (C2)
beyond the influence of sinners, and raised (C3)
27 up above the heavens; ·one who would not (C2)

need to offer sacrifices every day, as the other high priests do for their own sins and then for those of the people, because he has done 28 this once and for all by offering himself. •The Law appoints high priests who are men subject to weakness; but the promise on oath, which came after the Law, appointed the Son who is made perfect *for ever.*

B. THE SUPERIORITY OF THE WORSHIP, THE SANCTUARY AND THE MEDIATION PROVIDED BY CHRIST THE PRIEST

The new priesthood and the new sanctuary

1 8 The great point of all that we have said is that we have a high priest of exactly this kind. He has his place *at the right* of the 2 throne of divine Majesty in the heavens, •and he is the minister of the sanctuary and of the true *Tent* of Meeting which *the Lord,* and not 3 any man, *set up.*^a •It is the duty of every high priest to offer gifts and sacrifices, and so this 4 one too must have something to offer. •In fact, if he were on earth, he would not be a priest at all, since there are others who make 5 the offerings laid down by the Law •and these only maintain the service of a model or a reflection of the heavenly realities. For Moses, when he had the Tent to build, was warned by God who said: *See that you make everything according to the pattern shown you on the mountain.*^b

Christ is the mediator of a greater covenant

6 We have seen that he has been given a ministry of a far higher order, and to the same degree it is a better covenant of which he is the mediator, founded on better promises. 7 If that first covenant had been without a fault,

there would have been no need for a second
8 one to replace it. •And in fact God does find fault with them; he says:

See, the days are coming—it is the Lord who speaks—
when I will establish a new covenant
with the House of Israel and the House of Judah,
9 *but not a covenant like the one I made with their ancestors*

on the day I took them by the hand
to bring them out of the land of Egypt.
They abandoned that covenant of mine,
and so I on my side deserted them. It is the Lord who speaks.

10 *No, this is the covenant I will make*
with the House of Israel
when those days arrive—it is the Lord who speaks.
I will put my laws into their minds
and write them on their hearts.
Then I will be their God
and they shall be my people.

11 *There will be no further need for neighbor to try to teach neighbor,*
or brother to say to brother,
"Learn to know the Lord."
No, they will all know me,
the least no less than the greatest,
12 *since I will forgive their iniquities*
and never call their sins to mind.[c]

13 By speaking of a *new* covenant, he implies that the first one is already old. Now anything old only gets more antiquated until in the end it disappears.

Week 3 Day 4
Four C's Reflections
on Hebrews 6:1-8:13

1. Blessed Lord and Savior, in today's Scripture reading we encountered some very sobering words. We were told that those who accepted You and Your heavenly doctrine, and shared in Your divine life by the power of the Holy Spirit, but then fell away, cannot be brought back to Your friendship.[114] This utter rejection of You and Your saving grace was said to be a form of crucifying and mocking You.

2. Dearest Jesus, may we never lose our faith in You Who alone can save us from sin and everlasting death. May we never become so hardened in our sins that Your loving mercy and kindness can no longer reach us. May our hearts be always open to Your

inspirations to love You and to repent of our sinfulness, so that we can live in Your friendship now and in eternity. *(Some writers hold that the impossibility of being reconciled to God spoken of in Hebrews does not rule out the possibility of a special miraculous intervention of God's grace through which the hardened sinner can be restored to God's friendship.)*

3. Today's meditation also gives us hope, Lord, since we were assured our acts of charity will not be forgotten. "God would not be so unjust as to forget all you have done, the love that you have for his name or the services you have done, and are still doing, for the saints."[115]

4. Clearly, Lord, You reward those who love You and their fellow man, especially their fellow Christians. As a matter of fact, You and Your Catholic Church assure us the more we love You and others, for Your sake, the greater will be our reward of happiness and inner peace in Your heavenly presence.

5. Jesus, Our Lord, may we love You increasingly through Your divinely inspired thoughts, words and deeds, so we may be rewarded with an increasing capacity to enjoy Your goodness, truth and perfection.

6. Yet, Lord, no matter how holy we may become in this life, the possibility that we can lose our eternal inheritance always exists. Therefore we need to persevere in Your friendship and saving grace until the moment we die, as the following passage from today's reading teaches us.

7. "Our one desire is that every one of you should go on showing the same earnestness (in sowing seed-charity) to the end, to the perfect fulfillment of our hopes, never growing careless, but imitating those who have the faith and the perseverance to inherit the promises."(116)

8. Most Sacred Heart of Jesus, You know that remaining in Your friendship, day after day, is not easy. We are often faced with temptations to deny You. Yet we also realize that the same temptations, when resisted, are opportunities to grow in virtue and to know and love You more.

9. Thankfully, You always give us the grace to resist temptations when we seek it. With it, we can persevere each day in Your friendship. Also through the intercessions of Your most holy Mother, and all the saints, we receive help to remain steadfast in Your friendship until we die, and thus inherit Your promise of eternal salvation.

10. Lord, in today's meditation, You are described as the perfect, sinless, and eternal High Priest Who intercedes forever on our behalf. [117]

11. As our High Priest, You offer Yourself for us to the Father continuously as the perfect Victim Who takes away our sins. And through our participation in the Holy Sacrifice of the Mass and through the ministry of Your ordained priesthood, we enter into Your eternal sacrifice to the Father. In this unbloody Sacrifice of the Altar, as Your Catholic Church teaches, we plead together with You to the Father for the propitiation of our sins and the many other benefits of Your bloody sacrifice on the Cross. *(Propitiation is asking God to be merciful to us sinners and to mitigate or lighten the temporal punishment due to our sins. See "The Catholic Catechism," pp. 560-562, and p. 846 of the "Modern Catholic Dictionary.")*

12. "This sacrifice (of the Mass) is truly propitiatory, so that if we draw near to God with an upright heart and true faith, and with fear and reverence, with sorrow and repentance, through the Mass we may obtain mercy and find grace to help in time of need. For by this oblation the Lord is appeased. He grants grace and the gift of repentance, and he pardons wrong-doing and sins, even grave ones. The benefits of this oblation (the bloody one, that is) are received in abundance through this unbloody oblation. By no means, then, does the sacrifice of this Mass detract from the sacrifice of the cross.

13. "Therefore, the Mass may properly be offered according to Apostolic tradition for their sins, punishments, satisfaction, and other necessities of the faithful on earth, as well as for those who have died in Christ and are not yet wholly cleansed." *(The Ecumenical Council of Trent (1545-1563), — Denzinger 940. See also "The Catholic Catechism," p. 468.)*

14. Most loving and merciful Father, we deeply thank You for the eternal sacrifice of Your dear Son. Grant that we may so prepare ourselves for the celebration of the Holy Eucharist, that we may fruitfully enter into His sacrifice and obtain its many blessings for ourselves and others. We ask this through Jesus Christ, Our Lord and Savior. Amen.

Try to read these Scripture passages and meditations in a reflective manner every day. The Holy Spirit will reveal more insights to you each time you do so.

Please refer to Chapter XXIII, Paragraphs 1 to 4 and Chapter XXIV, Paragraphs 1 to 4 of our "Peaceful Seed Living" book, Volume II.

WEEK 3 DAY 5
Hebrews 9:1-10:39

Christ enters the heavenly sanctuary

9 The first covenant also had its laws governing worship, and its sanctuary, a sanctuary on this earth. ·There was a tent which comprised two compartments: the first, in which the lamp-stand, the table and the presentation loaves were kept, was called the Holy Place; ·then beyond the second veil, an innermost part which was called the Holy of Holies ·to which belonged the gold altar of incense, and the ark of the covenant, plated all over with gold. In this were kept the gold jar containing the manna, Aaron's branch that grew the buds, and the stone tablets of the covenant. ·On top of it was the throne of mercy, and outspread over it were the glorious cherubs. This is not the time to go into greater detail about this.

6 Under these provisions, priests are constantly going into the outer tent to carry out their acts of worship, ·but the second tent is entered only once a year, and then only by the high priest who must go in by himself and take the blood to offer for his own faults and the people's. ·By this, the Holy Spirit is showing that no one has the right to go into the sanctuary as long as the outer tent remains standing; ·it is a symbol for this present time.

None of the gifts and sacrifices offered under these regulations can possibly bring any worshiper to perfection in his inner self; ·they are rules about the outward life, connected with foods and drinks and washing at various times, intended to be in force only until it should be time to reform them.

11 But now Christ has come, as the high

priest of all the blessings which were to come. He has passed through the greater, the more perfect tent, which is better than the one made by men's hands because it is not
12 of this created order; •and he has entered the sanctuary once and for all, taking with him not the blood of goats and bull calves, but his own blood, having won an eternal redemp-
13 tion for us. •The blood of goats and bulls and the ashes of a heifer are sprinkled on those who have incurred defilement and they re- (C2)
14 store the holiness of their outward lives; •how (C2) much more effectively the blood of Christ, who offered himself as the perfect sacrifice

to God through the eternal Spirit, can purify our inner self from dead actions so (C2) that we do our service to the living God. (C3)

Christ seals the new covenant with his blood

15 He brings a new covenant, as the mediator, only so that the people who were called to an eternal inheritance may actually receive what was promised: his death took place to cancel the sins that infringed the earlier cove- (C2)
16 nant. •Now wherever a will is in question, the death of the testator must be established;
17 indeed, it only becomes valid with that death, since it is not meant to have any effect while
18 the testator is still alive. •That explains why even the earlier covenant needed something
19 to be killed in order to take effect, •and why, after Moses had announced all the commandments of the Law to the people, he took the calves' blood, the goats' blood and some water, and with these he sprinkled the book itself and all the people, using scarlet wool and
20 hyssop; •saying as he did so: *This is the blood of the covenant that God has laid down for*
21 *you.*[a] •After that, he sprinkled the tent and all

the liturgical vessels with blood in the same
22 way. •In fact, according to the Law almost everything has to be purified[b] with blood; and

if there is no shedding of blood, there is no
23 remission. ·Obviously, only the copies of heavenly things can be purified in this way, and the heavenly things themselves have to be purified by a higher sort of sacrifice than
24 this. ·It is not as though Christ had entered a man-made sanctuary which was only modeled on the real one; but it was heaven itself, so that he could appear in the actual presence
25 of God on our behalf. ·And he does not have to offer himself again and again, like the high priest going into the sanctuary year after year
26 with the blood that is not his own, ·or else he would have had to suffer over and over again since the world began. Instead of that, he has made his appearance once and for all, now at the end of the last age, to do away with
27 sin by sacrificing himself. ·Since men only (C2)
28 die once, and after that comes judgment, ·so Christ, too, offers himself only once *to take the faults of many on himself*,^c and when he (C2) appears a second time, it will not be to deal with sin but to reward with salvation those (C2) who are waiting for him. (C1) (C3)

SUMMARY: CHRIST'S SACRIFICE SUPERIOR TO THE SACRIFICES OF THE MOSAIC LAW

The old sacrifices ineffective

10 ¹So, since the Law has no more than a *reflection* of these realities, and no finished picture of them, it is quite incapable of bringing the worshipers to perfection, with the same sacrifices repeatedly offered year ²after year. ·Otherwise, the offering of them would have stopped, because the worshipers, when they had been purified once, would ³have no awareness of sins. ·Instead of that, the sins are recalled year after year in the ⁴sacrifices. ·Bulls' blood and goats' blood are ⁵useless for taking away sins, ·and this is what he said, on coming into the world:

You who wanted no sacrifice or oblation,
prepared a body for me.
⁶ *You took no pleasure in holocausts or sacrifices for sin;*

⁷ *then I said,*
  just as I was commanded in the scroll of the book,
  "God, here I am! I am coming to obey your will."[a]

8 Notice that he says first: *You did not want what the Law lays down as the things to be offered,* that is: *the sacrifices, the oblations, the holocausts and the sacrifices for sin,* and
9 *you took no pleasure* in them; ·and then he says: *Here I am! I am coming to obey your will.* He is abolishing the first sort to re-
10 place it with the second. ·And this *will* was for us to be made holy by the *offering* of his *body* made once and for all by Jesus Christ.

The efficacy of Christ's sacrifice

11 All the priests stand at their duties every day, offering over and over again the same sacrifices which are quite incapable of taking
12 sins away. ·He, on the other hand, has offered one single sacrifice for sins, and then taken his place for ever, *at the right hand of God,*
13 where he is now waiting *until his enemies are*
14 *made into a footstool for him.*[b] ·By virtue of that one single offering, he has achieved the eternal perfection of all whom he is sanctify-
15 ing. ·The Holy Spirit assures us of this; for he says, first:

16 *This is the covenant I will make with them when those days arrive;*[c]

and the Lord then goes on to say:

I will put my laws into their hearts and write them on their minds.
17 *I will never call their sins to mind, or their offenses.*

18 When all sins have been forgiven, there can be no more sin offerings.

IV. PERSEVERING FAITH

The Christian opportunity

19 In other words, brothers, through the

blood of Jesus we have the right to enter the
20 sanctuary, •by a new way which he has opened for us, a living opening through the
21 curtain, that is to say, his body. •And we have the *supreme high priest* over all *the house of*
22 *God*. •So as we go in, let us be sincere in heart and filled with faith, our minds sprinkled and free from any trace of bad conscience and our bodies washed with pure wa-
23 ter. •Let us keep firm in the hope we profess, because the one who made the promise is
24 faithful. •Let us be concerned for each other, to stir a response in love and good works.
25 Do not stay away from the meetings of the community, as some do, but encourage each other to go; the more so as you see the Day drawing near.

The danger of apostasy

26 If, after we have been given knowledge of the truth, we should deliberately commit any sins, then there is no longer any sacrifice for
27 them. •There will be left only the dreadful prospect of judgment and of *the raging fire*
28 that is to *burn rebels.*[d] •Anyone who disregards the Law of Moses is ruthlessly *put to death on the word of two witnesses or three;*[e]
29 and you may be sure that anyone who tramples on the Son of God, and who treats *the blood of the covenant* which sanctified him as if it were not holy, and who insults the Spirit of grace, will be condemned to a far severer
30 punishment. •We are all aware who it was that said: *Vengeance is mine; I will repay.*[f] And
31 again: *The Lord will judge his people.* •It is a dreadful thing to fall into the hands of the living God.

Motives for perseverance

32 Remember all the sufferings that you had to meet after you received the light, in earlier
33 days; •sometimes by being yourselves pub-

licly exposed to insults and violence, and sometimes as associates of others who were ³⁴ treated in the same way. •For you not only shared in the sufferings of those who were in prison, but you happily accepted being stripped of your belongings, knowing that you owned something that was better and ³⁵ lasting. •Be as confident now, then, since the ³⁶ reward is so great. •You will need endurance to do God's will and gain what he has promised.

³⁷ Only *a little while now, a very little while, and the one that is coming will have come; he will not delay.*ᵍ

³⁸ *The righteous man will live by faith, but if he draws back, my soul will take no pleasure in him.*ʰ

³⁹ You and I are not the sort of people who *draw back*, and are lost by it; we are the sort who keep *faithful* until our souls are saved.

Week 3 Day 5
Four C's Reflections
on Hebrews 9:1-10:39

1. Lord Jesus, in today's Scripture reading, Your high priesthood is again stressed. As our sinless High Priest, You sacrificed Your human life to the Father in order to restore us to our lost supernatural life.[118]

2. It was in this supernatural life that our first parents originally enjoyed God's presence and friendship. And since they had not yet experienced the curse of sin and death, they were heirs of the Kingdom of Heaven.

3. As we have noted in an earlier meditation, on account of the Fall, our first parents were excluded from the enjoyment of God's friendship, as were all their descendants.

4. In the course of centuries and in anticipation of Your sacrifice on the Cross, the Father chose certain people to experience His friendship in this life. But they were excluded from Your eternal Kingdom until You had, in Your own Body, broken the chains of sin and death.

5. Thus, Noah, Abraham, Moses and the Hebrew people, for example, were objects of God's special providential concern. They were chosen to prepare the world for Your Coming and for the salvation of all nations.

6. The Hebrews were specially chosen to know God and to learn His will. They were given the Law of Moses and a priesthood to

intercede for them through acts of sacrifice. Yet their sacrifices were incapable of restoring the gifts and graces lost at the time of the Fall. They could not remove human sinfulness, the chief barrier to the enjoyment of divine love.

7. Finally, in what St. Paul terms, "the appointed time",[119] You the eternal Son of the Father were sent to be the perfect, sinless High Priest Who would be able to remove the sins, not only of the Jews but of all people. Thus You effect in Your Church, through Your sacrifice on the Cross, a restoration to divine favor and friendship.

8. Furthermore, You established in Your Holy Catholic Church an ordained priesthood which participates in Your eternal high priesthood by offering up the Holy Sacrifice of the Mass and by administering the sacrament of Penance. In this way friendship with God is

continually renewed and strengthened, sins are forgiven, and the punishment due to sin is removed. *(For information regarding unremitted punishment due to sin, see the presentation on indulgences on pp. 561-565 of "The Catholic Catechism.")*

9. Lord, may we always highly value Your eternal high priesthood and honor those who are ordained to exercise it on behalf of the faithful. May they always properly administer Your sacraments. And may their lives reflect Your holiness, thereby attracting many souls to a saving relationship with You through Your Church.

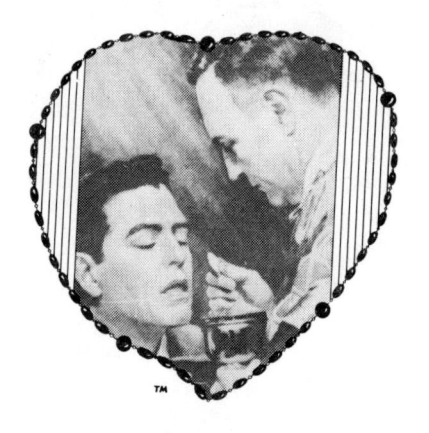

10. Yes, Jesus, You are our eternal High Priest, the perfect Mediator between God and man, Who makes possible even on earth life in the eternal Kingdom of Your Father. Yet, we must have the proper disposition to avail

ourselves of this heavenly life, as we learned in today's reading.

11. "In other words, brothers, through the blood of Jesus we have the right to enter the sanctuary, by a new way which he has opened for us, a living opening through the curtain, that is to say his body. And we have the supreme high priest over all the house of God. So as we go in, let us be sincere in heart and filled with faith, our minds sprinkled and free from any trace of bad conscience and our bodies washed with pure water. Let us keep firm in the hope we profess, because the one who made the promise is faithful. Let us be concerned for each other, to stir a response in love and good works. Do not stay away from the meetings of the community, as some do, but encourage each other to go."[120]

12. In order to enjoy divine charity and receive God's many gifts of blessings, we must be filled with faith, persevere in hope, have a pure conscience, and reflect our love for God in our active charity for one another. Lord, may this always be so.

13. Finally, Lord, we understand that those who first received the Letter to the Hebrews persevered in confidence and seed-charity in spite of suffering endured for their Faith. Their suffering included exposure to insults and violence, imprisonment, and the loss of worldly possessions.[121]

14. Lord, even today there are many who are suffering for their Faith and for their love

of You. We think especially of those who live in Communist countries throughout the world and those who suffer in the "free world" because of prejudice and pressure from certain non-Catholic elements within the Church itself.

15. Lord, may we never forget these brothers and sisters of ours. May we through our prayers and sacrifices, be channels of strength and comfort for them. And may their patient endurance in the midst of so many hardships encourage us to remain steadfast in Your friendship, especially when we too are faced with trials that sometimes seem unbearable. Amen.

Try to read these Scripture passages and meditations in a reflective manner every day. The Holy Spirit will reveal more insights to you each time you do so.

Please read and meditate on Chapter XXVI, Paragraphs 11 to 14, of "Peaceful Seed Living," Volume II.

WEEK 3 DAY 6
Hebrews 11:1-40

The exemplary faith of our ancestors

1 11 Only faith can guarantee the blessings that we hope for, or prove the existence of the realities that at present remain unseen.
2 It was for faith that our ancestors were commended.
3 It is by faith that we understand that the world was created by one word from God, so that no apparent cause can account for the things we can see.
4 It was because of his faith that Abel offered God a better sacrifice than Cain, and for that he was declared to be righteous when *God made acknowledgment of his offerings.* Though he is dead, he still speaks by faith.
5 It was because of his faith that Enoch was taken up and did not have to experience death: *he was not to be found because God had taken him.*[a] This was because before his assumption it is attested that *he had pleased*
6 *God.* ·Now it is impossible to please God without faith, since anyone who comes to him must believe that he exists and rewards those who try to find him.
7 It was through his faith that Noah, when he had been warned by God of something that had never been seen before, felt a holy fear and built an ark to save his family. By his faith the world was convicted, and he was able to claim the righteousness which is the reward of faith.
8 It was by faith that Abraham obeyed the call to *set out* for a country that was the inheritance given to him and his descendants, and that *he set out* without knowing where he
9 was going. ·By faith he arrived, *as a foreigner,* in the Promised Land, and lived there

as if in a strange country, with Isaac and Jacob, who were heirs with him of the same
10 promise. ·They lived there in tents while he looked forward to a city founded, designed and built by God.

11 It was equally by faith that Sarah, in spite of being past the age, was made able to conceive, because she believed that he who had made the promise would be faithful to it. (C1)

12 Because of this, there came from one man, and one who was already as good as dead himself, *more descendants than could be counted, as many as the stars of heaven or the grains of sand on the seashore.*[b]

13 All these died in faith, before receiving any of the things that had been promised, but they saw them in the far distance and welcomed them, recognizing that they were only *stran-*
14 *gers and nomads on earth.* ·People who use such terms about themselves make it quite plain that they are in search of their real
15 homeland. ·They can hardly have meant the country they came from, since they had the
16 opportunity to go back to it; ·but in fact they were longing for a better homeland, their heavenly homeland. That is why God is not ashamed to be called their God, since he has founded the city for them.

17 It was by faith that Abraham, *when put to the test, offered up Isaac.^c* He offered to sacrifice his only son even though the promises
18 had been made to him •and he had been told: *It is through Isaac that your name will be
19 carried on.^d* •He was confident that God had the power even to raise the dead; and so, figuratively speaking, he was given back Isaac from the dead.

20 It was by faith that this same Isaac gave his blessing to Jacob and Esau for the still
21 distant future. •By faith Jacob, when he was dying, blessed each of Joseph's sons, *leaning on the end of his stick as though bowing to
22 pray.^e* •It was by faith that, when he was about to die, Joseph recalled the Exodus of the Israelites and made the arrangements for his own burial.

23 It was by faith that Moses, when he was born, *was hidden by his parents for three months;* they defied the royal edict when they
24 *saw* he was such a *fine* child. •It was by faith that, *when he grew to manhood,* Moses re-
25 fused to be known as the son of Pharaoh's daughter •and chose to be ill-treated in company with God's people rather than to enjoy

26 for a time the pleasures of sin. •He considered that the insults offered to the Anointed were something more precious than all the treasures of Egypt, because he had his eyes
27 fixed on the reward. •It was by faith that he left Egypt and was not afraid of the king's anger; he held to his purpose like a man who
28 could see the Invisible. •It was by faith that he kept *the Passover* and sprinkled *the blood* to prevent *the Destroyer* from touching any
29 of the firstborn sons of Israel. •It was by faith they crossed the Red Sea as easily as dry land, while the Egyptians, trying to do the same, were drowned.

30 It was through faith that the walls of Jericho fell down when the people had been

31 round them for seven days. •It was by faith (C1)
that Rahab the prostitute welcomed the
spies and so was not killed with the unbe- (C2)
lievers.

32 Is there any need to say more? There is not
time for me to give an account of Gideon,
Barak, Samson, Jephthah, or of David, Sam-
33 uel and the prophets. •These were men who
through faith conquered kingdoms, did what (C1)
is right and earned the promises. They could
34 keep a lion's mouth shut, •put out blazing
fires and emerge unscathed from battle. They
were weak people who were given strength,
to be brave in war and drive back foreign
35 invaders. •Some came back to their wives
from the dead, by resurrection; and others
submitted to torture, refusing release so that (C2)
36 they would rise again to a better life. •Some
had to bear being pilloried and flogged, or (C2)
37 even chained up in prison. •They were
stoned, or sawn in half,*f* or beheaded; they (C2)
were homeless, and dressed in the skins of
sheep and goats; they were penniless and
38 were given nothing but ill-treatment. •They (C2)
were too good for the world and they went (C3)
out to live in deserts and mountains and in
39 caves and ravines. •These are all heroes of
faith, but they did not receive what was prom- (C1)
40 ised, •since God had made provision for us
to have something better, and they were not
to reach perfection except with us.

223

Week 3 Day 6
Four C's Reflections
on Hebrews 11:1-40

1. Most Sacred Heart of Jesus, the theological virtue of faith is the theme which runs throughout today's meditation. As Your Church teaches, this grace enables our minds, in cooperation with our wills, to assent firmly to all the truths revealed by God for our salvation.

2. Because of Your sacrificial death, Lord, You merited faith for all mankind, even for those, as our mediation illustrates, who lived before Your Coming. Moreover, faith is active in all people, Christians or not, who believe both in God's existence and that He rewards those who seek to please Him.[122]

3. We Catholics should not take this to mean, however, that because many non-Christians and many non-Catholic Christians possess faith, we have no obligation to enlighten them further. While it is true that such persons may well be on their way to salvation, we who have a greater knowledge and understanding of God's revelation have a duty to share this great treasure with them.

4. In the closing words of St. Matthew's Gospel, for instance, You told Your Apostles to make disciples of all people, to baptize them and to teach them to observe all Your commandments. It would be nothing less than selfish, Lord, to deliberately deny to one of our fellow humans the full knowledge of

Your saving revelation which has been entrusted to the safe-keeping of Your Holy Catholic Church.

5. Sometimes, it is argued that there are many roads to salvation and we should not disturb the "good faith" of others. In fact, however, there is only one road to salvation, namely You, Who are the Way, the Truth and the Life[123] St. Peter expressed this great truth when he proclaimed, "For of all the names in the world given to men, this is the only one by which we can be saved."[124]

6. This does not mean, of course, that those who do not explicitly know You cannot be saved. It means only that You alone are their Savior whether they realize it or not. But, to keep people deliberately in ignorance of this fact is certainly not an act of charity. Consequently, we should share the fullness of Your revelation with those willing to listen, doing it with a measure of tact, gentleness, and respect for their sincerely held beliefs.

7. Lord, today's Scripture reading reminds us of many who possessed deep faith during the Old Testament period. Enoch, for example, on account of his faith, did not experience death, but was "taken up." We should not, however, take this to mean that he preceded Your entry into heavenly glory.

8. Our Scripture reading also asked us to consider Noah who was contrasted with the sinners who perished in the Flood. It would appear the essential difference was that Noah was saved by his faith, while the others

drowned because of their lack of faith. Furthermore, Noah by his faith was rewarded with the gift of righteousness which included divine friendship. *(For a definition of the gift of righteousness or justification, see the entries, "Justification, Theology of" and "Justifying Grace" on pp. 301-302 of the "Modern Catholic Dictionary.")*

9. Lord, may we never lack the gift of faith, which together with seed-charity, leads to righteousness and everlasting life. And through our prayers and other acts of charity, grant the virtue of faith to those among our friends and acquaintances who do not yet possess it.

10. Jesus, we were also given the example of the faith of Abraham and Sarah, through which they did great things for mankind in their old age. Their strong faith reminds us that we too can use this gift to accomplish

great things for mankind. We can be channels of grace through our prayers for others. And we can share with those who have not yet received it, the Good News of man's salvation. Moreover, through our faith, we can be motivated to protect the unborn, the poor, and the mentally and physically handicapped.

11. Lord, let us never forget the faith of Moses, through which he spurned a life of luxury to spend forty years of hardship in the wilderness, leading his often rebellious people to their destiny in Canaan. May his faith inspire us to regard ourselves — as Scripture urges — as pilgrims and strangers in the "wilderness" of the entire world, seeking our destiny not on earth but in Heaven. [125]

12. Lord, the examples of those who possessed great faith during the Old Testament era give us comfort, and encourage us to always exercise our faith. But as You well know, we also have in our own Christian era, examples of deep and abiding faith in You. This was particularly true among the saints.

13. By their faith (and charity) thousands were converted to Catholicism, Religious communities were founded, vocations to the priesthood and Religious life were multiplied, families were blessed, evil forces were defeated and schools and hospitals were established.

14. Even today, Jesus, those who have

faith are "moving mountains" and accomplishing "impossible" dreams. We think in particular of those who are spiritually renewing Your Church in the presence of fierce opposition in both totalitarian and "free" countries. And there are those also who have given up completely the so-called "good life" in the world in order to serve You and their fellow humans more perfectly. Furthermore, there are many faithful individuals leading heroic lives of sanctity in the world. They include bishops, priests, deacons, parents, teachers, members of Religious communities, and lay leaders. These are bringing many to You through Your Holy Catholic Church. Nor should we forget those heroic non-Catholic Christians who serve You so well as members of their respective Churches and religious communities.

15. For these, we offer thanks, Lord. Grant that we may never hesitate to imitate their faith and charity, thereby drawing ever closer to You and to the peace of God which surpasses all understanding.[126] Amen.

Try to read these Scripture passages and meditations in a reflective manner every day. The Holy Spirit will reveal more insights to you each time you do so.

Please refer to Chapter XXVII, Paragraphs 1 to 4 of our "Peaceful Seed Living" book, Volume II.

WEEK 3 DAY 7
Hebrews 12:1-13:25

The example of Jesus Christ

12 ¹With so many witnesses in a great cloud on every side of us, we too, then, should throw off everything that hinders us, especially the sin that clings so easily, and (C1) keep running steadily in the race we have (C4) ²started. ·Let us not lose sight of Jesus, who leads us in our faith and brings it to perfec- (C1) tion: for the sake of the joy which was still in the future, he endured the cross, disregarding the shamefulness of it, and *from now on has taken his place at the right* of God's ³throne. ·Think of the way he stood such opposition from sinners and then you will not (C1) ⁴give up for want of courage. ·In the fight against sin, you have not yet had to keep (C2) fighting to the point of death. (C4)

God's fatherly instruction

⁵ Have you forgotten that encouraging text in which you are addressed as sons? *My son, when the Lord corrects you, do not treat it*

lightly; but do not get discouraged when he
6 *reprimands you.* ·*For the Lord trains the ones that he loves and he punishes all those that*
7 *he acknowledges as his sons.*[a] ·Suffering is part of your *training;* God is treating you as his *sons.* Has there ever been any *son* whose
8 father did not *train* him? ·If you were not getting this training, as all of you are, then

9 you would not be *sons* but bastards. ·Besides, we have all had our human fathers who punished us, and we respected them for it; we ought to be even more willing to submit ourselves to our spiritual Father, to be given life. (C3)
10 Our human fathers were thinking of this short life when they punished us, and could only do what they thought best; but he does it all for our own good, so that we may share his
11 own holiness. ·Of course, any punishment is most painful at the time, and far from pleasant; but later, in those on whom it has been used, it bears fruit in peace and
12 goodness. ·So *hold up your limp arms and*
13 *steady your trembling knees*[b] ·and *smooth out the path you tread;*[c] then the injured limb will not be wrenched, it will grow strong again.

Unfaithfulness is punished

14   *Always be wanting peace*[d] with all people, (C3)
    and the holiness without which no one can (C2)
15 ever see the Lord. ·Be careful that no one is deprived of the grace of God and that no *root* (C2)

   of bitterness should begin to grow and make (C2)
   trouble;[e] this can poison a whole community.
16 And be careful that there is no immorality, (C2)
   or that any of you does not degrade religion (C2)
   like Esau, *who sold his birthright* for one
17 single meal. ·As you know, when he wanted to obtain the blessing afterward, he was rejected and, though he pleaded for it with tears, he was unable to elicit a change of heart.

230

The two covenants

18 What you have come to is nothing known to the senses: not a *blazing fire,*[f] or a *gloom*
19 *turning to total darkness,* or a *storm;* or *trumpeting thunder* or the *great voice speaking* which made everyone that heard it beg that
20 no more should be said to them. ·They were appalled at the order that was given: *If even an animal touches the mountain, it must be*
21 *stoned.* ·The whole scene was so terrible that Moses said: *I am afraid,*[g] and was trembling
22 with fright. ·But what you have come to is Mount Zion and the city of the living God, the heavenly Jerusalem where the millions of
23 angels have gathered for the festival, ·with the whole Church in which everyone is a "firstborn son" and a citizen of heaven. You have come to God himself, the supreme Judge, and been placed with the spirits of the
24 saints who have been made perfect; ·and to Jesus, the mediator who brings a new covenant and a blood for purification which pleads
25 more insistently than Abel's. ·Make sure that you never refuse to listen when he speaks. The people who refused to listen to the warning from a voice on earth could not escape their punishment, and how shall we escape if we turn away from a voice that warns us
26 from heaven? ·That time his voice made the earth shake, but now he has given us this promise: *I shall make the earth shake once more and* not only the earth but *heaven as*
27 *well.*[h] ·The words *once more* show that since the things being shaken are created things, they are going to be changed, so that the
28 unshakeable things will be left. ·We have been given possession of an unshakable kingdom. Let us therefore hold on to the grace that we have been given and use it to worship God in the way that he finds acceptable,
29 in reverence and fear. ·For our *God is a consuming fire.*[i]

APPENDIX

Final recommendations

¹ **13**² Continue to love each other like brothers, ·and remember always to welcome strangers, for by doing this, some people have entertained angels without knowing it. ³ Keep in mind those who are in prison, as though you were in prison with them; and those who are being badly treated, since you ⁴ too are in the one body. ·Marriage is to be honored by all, and marriages are to be kept undefiled, because fornicators and adulterers ⁵ will come under God's judgment. ·Put greed out of your lives and be content with whatever you have; God himself has said: *I will* ⁶ *not fail you or desert you,*^a ·and so we can say with confidence: *With the Lord to help me, I fear nothing: what can man do to me?*^b

Faithfulness

⁷ Remember your leaders, who preached the word of God to you, and as you reflect on the outcome of their lives, imitate their ⁸ faith. ·Jesus Christ is the same today as he

9 was yesterday and as he will be for ever. Do not let yourselves be led astray by all sorts of strange doctrines: it is better to rely on (C2) grace for inner strength than on dietary laws which have done no good to those who kept
10 them. We have our own altar from which those who serve the tabernacle have no right
11 to eat. The bodies of the animals *whose blood is brought into the sanctuary* by the high priest *for the atonement of sin are burned*
12 *outside the camp*,^c and so Jesus too suffered outside the gate to sanctify the people with
13 his own blood. Let us go to him, then, *out-*
14 *side the camp,* and share his degradation. For (C3) there is no eternal city for us in this life but
15 we look for one in the life to come. Through him, *let us offer God* an unending *sacrifice of praise*,^d a verbal sacrifice that is offered (C3)
16 every time we acknowledge his name. Keep (C1) doing good works and sharing your re- (C3)(C4)

sources, for these are sacrifices that please God.

Obedience to religious leaders

17 Obey your leaders and do as they tell you, (C3) because they must give an account of the way they look after your souls; make this a joy for (C3) them to do, and not a grief—you yourselves
18 would be the losers. We are sure that our own conscience is clear and we are certainly (C2) determined to behave honorably in every- (C3)
19 thing we do; pray for us. I ask you very (C3) particularly to pray that I may come back to (C3) you all the sooner.

EPILOGUE

News, good wishes and greetings

20 I pray that the God of peace, *who brought* (C3) our Lord Jesus *back*^e from the dead *to become the great Shepherd of the sheep*^f *by*

*the blood that sealed an eternal covenant,*ᵍ
21 may make you ready to do his will in any kind (C3)
of good action; and turn us all into whatever
is acceptable to himself through Jesus Christ,
to whom be glory for ever and ever, Amen.

22 I do ask you, brothers, to take these words
of advice kindly; that is why I have written (C3)
to you so briefly.

23 I want you to know that our brother
Timothy has been set free. If he arrives in
time, he will be with me when I see you.

24 Greetings to all your leaders and to all the (C3)
saints. The saints of Italy send you greetings. (C3)

25 Grace be with you all. (C3)

Week 3 Day 7
Four C's Reflections
on Hebrews 12:1-13:25

1. Most Sacred Heart of Jesus, in this our last meditation, St. Paul compares the life of sanctity to a race in which endurance to the end is essential, if a prize is to be obtained. Moreover, we were urged to imitate the innumerable holy ones of the past who successfully finished the race to Heaven by persevering in faith and by removing the obstacles of sin which they encountered along the way.(127)

2. Most importantly, St. Paul encouraged us in our daily race toward the Beatific Vision to keep Your example of perfect constancy always in mind. *(For more on the Beatific Vision in Heaven, see "The Catholic Catechism," pp. 260-263.)*

3. "For the sake of the joy which was still in the future, he endured the cross, disregarding the shamefulness of it, and from now on has taken his place at the right of God's throne. Think of the way he stood such opposition from sinners and then you will not give up for want of courage."(128)

4. Jesus, You are not only our perfect Model of sanctity Who successfully persevered in running the race to heavenly glory, but You are also the Source of any sanctity we may possess and the Source of the graces we need to achieve our eternal destiny. For this we thank You and praise You. We also thank You for the holy examples of Your Blessed

Mother, St. Joseph, the holy Apostles and all the saints.

5. Most Merciful Lord, our meditation also reminds us that unlike You and Your blessed martyrs, we have not yet had to fight sin to the point of yielding up our lives.[129] This truth puts us to shame since we have often yielded to temptation rather than suffering and resisting it.

6. Yet we must continually realize that You, in Your infinite goodness, will allow us to suffer at times to accomplish Your will, since it gives us the opportunity to prove we are Your true friends and worthy heirs of Your Kingdom.[130]

7. Lord, the following words in our meditation caught our attention since they can readily be applied to parents and families.

8. "Always be wanting peace with all people, and the holiness without which no one can ever see the Lord. Be careful that no one is deprived of the grace of God and that

no root of bitterness should begin to grow and make trouble; this can poison a whole community."[131]

9. How important it is for family well-being, Jesus, that peace, charity and holiness should reign within the setting of the home. Yet, in fact, fighting and selfishness often prevail. The family can be a training ground for either sanctity or self-centeredness. If sanctity prevails, so do peace and charity. If self-centeredness predominates, disharmony and bitterness are its inevitable fruit, poisoning the whole family, and sometimes future generations as well.

10. Parents have the greater responsibility for cultivating peace and sanctity at home. Yet we know there are times when it is very difficult to bring these about. Nevertheless, starting with themselves they must always try.

11. Actually, the task would be much simpler if husbands and wives would be models of holiness in their dealings with one another. Thus, examples would be provided for their children to imitate in their own relationships with their parents and among themselves. But, as we well know, they cannot do this properly without the aid of divine grace in their lives. Therefore, as our Scripture reading implicitly warns, parents should not deprive their children of Your supernatural help[132] Consequently, they need to learn how to pray individually and with the family. And they need to be exposed to the grace and proper use of the sacraments.

12. Lord, by the power of Your Holy Spirit, inspire Christian parents to draw daily upon the grace of Matrimony. Consequently, they will be able to love one another deeply as spouses and act in peace and harmony with one another, and be models of Christian conduct for their children.

13. Jesus, we have already noted where St. Paul compared the Christian life to a race in which perseverance was rewarded with a prize. And we encountered a similar thought in the following words of today's Scripture reading: "We have been given possession of an unshakeable kingdom. Let us therefore hold onto the grace that we have been given and use it to worship God in the way that he finds acceptable, in reverence and fear."[133]

14. Yes, Lord, continued membership in God's Kingdom, while we live on earth,

depends upon our willingness to hold on and to make use of the grace we have so generously been given in Your Church. We are to use this grace to worship God and confide in Him with a pure heart. In return, we shall receive not only continued membership in His Kingdom, but also His blessings of interior peace and happiness. *(For a description of the Church as the earthly and heavenly Kingdom of God, see p. 209 of "The Catholic Catechism.")*

15. Lord, grant us the grace of constancy so we may persevere to the end in God's friendship and inherit eternal life in His Kingdom. May His Kingdom come and may His will always be done on earth as it is in Heaven.

16. Finally, Lord Jesus, we wish to reflect a few moments on one sentence in today's meditation which has particular relevance for those who are married. "Marriage is to honored by all, and marriages are to be kept undefiled, because fornicators and adulterers will come under God's judgment."[134]

17. Jesus, perhaps never before in the history of Christianity has marriage been taken so lightly on such a vast scale. In some areas of our country, for instance, the annual number of divorces is about the same as the annual number of new marriages. And such widespread disregard for the sanctity of marriage bears bitter fruit indeed. Clearly, one of the greatest factors contributing to the ills of our society is the breaking of marriage vows.

18. Lord, the sanctity, the life-long permanence, and grave responsibilities of marriage must be taught today with renewed vigor and clarity by bishops, priests, Religious and parents, if our society is to be once more genuinely Christian. Inspire married couples to turn to You for help when things go wrong between themselves rather than turning to lawyers, divorce courts and marriage tribunals.

19. In order to avoid serious marital difficulties, it is necessary for spouses to pray together daily. They should pray for themselves and for their marriage and family, with the knowledge that You are an essential partner in their marriage Who will guarantee its stability and well-being, if Your help is sought. Always impress upon spouses that marriage is life-long, no matter what difficulties they may encounter or teaching they may hear to the contrary.

20. Continually grant to spouses, Lord, and to their children, confidence in You, freedom from sin and a charitable relationship with God and all others, especially with the members of their own families. Amen.

Try to read these Scripture passages and meditations in a reflective manner every day. The Holy Spirit will reveal more insights to you each time you do so.

Try to read and meditate on Chapter XXVIII, Paragraphs 1 to 3 and Chapter XXIX of "Peaceful Seed Living," Volume II.

Scripture References

(1) Colossians 1:3-9
(2) Ephesians 6:19
(3) Colossians 1:23
(4) Colossians 1:29
(5) Colossians 1:28
(6) Colossians 1:9-10
(7) Colossians 2:8
(8) Colossians 3:1
(9) Colossians 3:2-3
(10) Colossians 3:5
(11) Colossians 3:3
(12) Colossians 3:13
(13) Ephesians 4:28
(14) Colossians 4:5-6
(15) I Thessalonians 1:9
(16) I Thessalonians 2:7
(17) Matthew 23:37
(18) I Thessalonians 2:11-12
(19) Colossians 2:8
(20) I Thessalonians 2:13
(21) I Thessalonians 3:1-5
(22) John 16:2-3
(23) Matthew 5:11-12
(24) Acts 5:41; 5:27-33
(25) Matthew 10:36
(26) Luke 6:23; Matthew 5:11-12
(27) I Thessalonians 3:12
(28) I Thessalonians 4:1
(29) I Thessalonians 5:13
(30) 2 Thessalonians 1:3-4
(31) 2 Thessalonians 1:5
(32) I Peter 1:7
(33) Matthew 10:22

(34) 2 Thessalonians 2:13
(35) Ephesians 1:5;1:11
(36) 2 Thessalonians 3:6-15
(37) Genesis 1:28; 2:15; 3:19
(38) 2 Thessalonians 3:15
(39) I Timothy 1:3-4
(40) I Timothy 1:12-16
(41) Acts 9:2; Galatians 1:13; 1 Corinthians 15:9
(42) I Timothy 1:16
(43) I Timothy 2:1-2
(44) I Timothy 3:2
(45) I Corinthians 7:32-35
(46) I Timothy 3:4, 12
(47) I Timothy 4:4-5
(48) I Timothy 4:10
(49) I Timothy 2:4-5
(50) Romans 10:14-15
(51) I Timothy 4:16
(52) I Timothy 5:1-8
(53) I Timothy 1:9
(54) I Timothy 5:2
(55) I Timothy 5:5
(56) I Timothy 5:21
(57) Galatians 2:6
(58) I Timothy 5:6
(59) I Timothy 6:3
(60) John 3:5
(61) I Timothy 6:7-10
(62) Colossians 3:5-6
(63) I Timothy 6:17
(64) Luke 12:15
(65) I Timothy 6:18-19
(66) Matthew 6:33
(67) 2 Timothy 1:3
(68) I Corinthians 4:3-4

(69) 2 Timothy 1:12
(70) 2 Timothy 1:8
(71) Luke 9:26
(72) Matthew 25:14-30
(73) Luke 9:23-34
(74) 2 Timothy 2:1
(75) 2 Timothy 2:2
(76) 2 Timothy 2:11-13
(77) 2 Timothy 4:2-5
(78) 2 Timothy 4:2-5
(79) 2 Timothy 4:3-4
(80) 2 Timothy 3:1-5
(81) 2 Timothy 3:12
(82) John 3:19
(83) 2 Corinthians 1:5
(84) 2 Timothy 3:15
(85) 2 Timothy 3:16
(86) Titus 1:2
(87) Psalm 88:10-12
(88) Psalm 88:3-5
(89) John 14:1-4
(90) Titus 1:6
(91) Titus 1:15
(92) Matthew 5:8
(93) Titus 2:2
(94) Titus 2:4
(95) Titus 2:11
(96) Titus 3:1
(97) I Peter 2:13-15
(98) Acts 5:29
(99) Titus 3:4-5
(100) Philemon 4
(101) Ephesians 6:18
(102) John 15:17
(103) Matthew 5:44
(104) Hebrews 1:1-3

(105) Hebrews 1:14
(106) Hebrews 2:3
(107) Hebrews 3:12-14
(108) Matthew 18:6-7
(109) Hebrews 4:1
(110) Hebrews 4:14-16
(111) John 15:13
(112) Hebrews 5:7-10
(113) Hebrews 5:11-14
(114) Hebrews 6:4-6
(115) Hebrews 6:10
(116) Hebrews 6:11-12
(117) Hebrews 6:19-20; 7:23-25
(118) Hebrews 9:11-14, 26-28; 10:10-20
(119) Galatians 4:4
(120) Hebrews 10:19-25
(121) Hebrews 10:32-35
(122) Hebrews 11:6
(123) John 14:6
(124) Acts 4:12
(125) I Peter 1:3-9; 2:11; Colossians 3:1-4
(126) Philippians 4:7
(127) Hebrews 12:1
(128) Hebrews 12:2-3
(129) Hebrews 12:4
(130) Matthew 10:38-39; Romans 8:17-18
Hebrews 12:7-13
(131) Hebrews 12:14-15
(132) Hebrews 12:15
(133) Hebrews 12:28
(134) Hebrews 13:4

The Work and Goals of the Apostolate

Purpose

The Apostolate for Family Consecration is an international community of believers whose specific purpose and unique role in the Church is to reinforce the Christian family through the systematic transformation of neighborhoods into God-centered communities. As a result of the establishment of enough of these "God-centered communities," a nation will advance significantly on the spiritual plane, and in most instances, even on the material level. "Virtue makes a nation great, by sin whole races are disgraced." *Proverbs 14:34)* "Happy is the nation whose God is the Lord."*(Psalms 33:12)* "...Bad friends ruin the noblest of people." *(I Cor. 15:33)*

Motto

All for the Sacred and Eucharistic Heart of Jesus, all through the Sorrowful and Immaculate Heart of Mary, all in union with St. Joseph.

Spirituality

The four biblical pillars of the Apostolate's "Peaceful Seed Living" spirituality are Confidence, Conscience, seed-Charity and Constancy. When a person builds his or her daily life on these four pillars, he or she will be living a life of true union with God and will be blessed with a peaceful heart that only God can give.

Our spiritual goal is to develop a deep interior union with the Holy Spirit of God. The best way to achieve this mystical union is by increasing not the number of prayers said but the fervor and time invested in prayer and meditation every day. When we convert our daily trials encountered through the fulfillment of our responsibilities into sacrifices for God, we actually unite ourselves with Christ's sacrifice of the Mass at Calvary. Only through these spiritual means, can we restore man's relationship with God and loosen the diabolical hold the forces of evil have on so many families, schools, neighborhoods, our country and the entire world.

Act of Consecration

The Act of Total Consecration to the Holy Family which the Apostolate promotes, offers all of a person's spiritual and material possessions for the Sacred and Eucharistic Heart of Jesus, through the Sorrowful and Immaculate Heart of Mary, in union with St. Joseph.

Through this act of total consecration, individuals are asking to be purified and used as God's instruments by the Holy Family. It is recognized that the Holy Family can do far more good with people's humble possessions than they ever could on their own. We believe that this offering enables God to multiply an individual's merits and offset the effects of sin in the world. *(2 Cor. 9:10)*

People who are totally consecrated give all of their indulgences to the Holy Family to relieve the suffering of loved ones and other Poor Souls in Purgatory. The Poor Souls are asked to continually pray that all the members of our families and the members and families of the Apostolate fulfill, to the fullest extent, the Father's distinctive plan for their lives.

Our Cooperator, Chapter and Apostolic members are required to make this act of total consecration. Other members and individuals who participate in our "Neighborhood Peace of Heart Forums" are encouraged, but not required, to also totally consecrate themselves to the Holy Family.

The Church's Guide and Incentive for Holiness

The Apostolate uses the Church's norms for indulgences as a specific guide for achieving a balanced, God-centered life in the modern world, while asking its members to perform heroic acts of charity by giving their indulgences to the Poor Souls in purgatory.

Neighborhood Chapter Programs

Our goal, God willing, is to establish, within every nation, a national network of Neighborhood Chapters capable of continually educating and motivating people to place God first in their lives. These chapters will perform four distinct functions:

• Change personal attitudes of neighborhood residents through in-depth and continuous "Neighborhood Peace of Heart Forums."

• Deepen personal commitment and effectiveness through total consecration to the Holy Family through our home visitation programs.

• Consolidate neighborhoods through public devotions in our churches.

• Cultivate our youth through our youth leadership programs.

When Chapters are Established

After enough Neighborhood Chapters are established in an area, the Apostolate will utilize the media as a positive means to draw people into our in-depth formation programs. We will also establish, within the area, a combination audio-visual lending library, religious book store and gift shop operated by our members.

Types of Membership

Membership is open to all who qualify and fulfill the following conditions:

A. Sacri-State members are those who offer up as a sacrifice of their state in life, their trials encountered in the faithful fulfillment of their responsibilities. They recognize the fact these sacrifices are not only meritorious, but if specifically willed, are also indulgenced by the Church.

Sacri-State members freely entrust either part or all of their merits and indulgences, earned from their prayers and sacrifices, to be distributed by the Holy Family. The Holy Family is asked to apply the merits of the members toward the work of the Apostolate, and to apply their indulgences for their loved ones and other Poor Souls in Purgatory.

We ask the Poor Souls helped by our indulgences to continually pray that all the members and families of the Apostolate fulfill the Father's distinctive plan for their lives. This commitment need only be made once and may be revoked by a specific act of the will at any time. Sacri-State members do not have to totally consecrate themselves to the Holy Family.

Sacri-State membership is a spiritual bond and, therefore, no formal application is necessary. One need only submit a note indicating a willingness to fulfill these conditions. There are also no dues for Sacri-State members.

If you belong to a religious community or an organized apostolic group, your entire community can join and become a Sacri-State community of the Apostolate.

B. Cooperator members are those who fulfill the conditions for Sacri-State membership, and also totally consecrate themselves to the Holy Family, and strive to follow the recommended practices, and recite the recommended prayers of the Apostolate for Family Consecration.

In addition, to become a Cooperator member, one should send for our formal application form and submit it for certification. Cooperator members may also be candidates for the following Apostolic or Chapter memberships.

C. Chapter members are those who are totally consecrated to the Holy Family and have successfully completed our candidate program, while actively working in the Apostolate on a voluntary basis.

D. Apostolic members are those who are totally consecrated to the Holy Family and have successfully completed our candidate program, while having committed themselves to devote at least one year in the work of the Apostolate on a full time basis.

E. Benefactor members are those individuals who contribute the much needed financial assistance to the Apostolate for Family Consecration. One may be a Benefactor member and also one of the other mentioned members.

Benefits of Membership

In unity there is strength. Our living and deceased members and their families will be remembered in all of the Masses offered for the Apostolate and its work.

In addition, all living and deceased members and their families will be remembered through the perpetual vigil lights in the sanctuary of the Sacred Hearts Chapel at the House of St. Joseph.

All members of the Apostolate are actually part of a community of believers who share in the prayers and merits of the other members throughout the world. We particularly ask our members to pray on Fridays for the specific petitions sent in to the Apostolate.

St. Paul said: "The more you sow, the more you reap." *(2 Cor. 9:6)* When you pray for others, you plant a seed of love that will bear an abundant harvest for your loved ones, yourselves and the entire Mystical Body of Christ.

All members who have been properly enrolled and wear the Brown Scapular, or Scapular medal of Our Lady of Mount Carmel, qualify for the Sabbatine Privilege and share in the combined good works of the entire Carmelite Order throughout the world and over 200 million members of the Scapular Confraternity.

Those who become associated with one of our neighborhood chapters will also receive the companionship and support of individuals holding like moral and spiritual convictions. In addition, our members will receive the great satisfaction of being able to make both their spiritual and temporal efforts count through their development of truly God-centered communities, which will nourish sound moral families in their local areas.

Those members who consecrate themselves totally to the Holy Family (to Jesus, through Mary, in union with St. Joseph) will receive an abundance of grace by becoming the Holy Family's consecrated children.

Those who donate their time and resources to the Apostolate will receive many partial indulgences for their good works.

All members of the Apostolate are spiritually united with Mother Teresa of Calcutta and all Missionaries of Charity throughout the world. On April 22, 1978, Mother Teresa, who is a member of our Advisory Council, signed up all of the members of her community as Sacri-State members of the Apostolate for Family Consecration. Therefore, all members of the Apostolate are spiritually united with Mother Teresa's community, and many other communities and generous individuals throughout the world, who are praying and suffering for our work. Indeed, when you combine this powerhouse of prayer and sacrifice with the prayers of the many souls being released from Purgatory because of our practices, our goal to be used as an instrument of the Holy Family to transform neighborhoods into God-centered communities will certainly be accomplished.

Litany of the Sacred Heart of Jesus

L. Lord, have mercy on us.
A. Christ, have mercy on us.

L. Lord, have mercy on us.
Christ, hear us.
A. Christ, graciously hear us.

God, the Father of Heaven,	*Have mercy on us.*
God the Son, Redeemer of the world,	*Have mercy on us.*
God the Holy Ghost,	*Have mercy on us.*
Holy Trinity, one God,	*Have mercy on us.*
Heart of Jesus, Son of the Eternal Father,	*Have mercy on us.*
Heart of Jesus, formed by the Holy Ghost in the Virgin Mother's womb,	*Have mercy on us.*
Heart of Jesus, substantially united to the Word of God,	*Have mercy on us.*

Heart of Jesus, of infinite majesty, *Have mercy on us.*

Heart of Jesus, holy temple of God, *Have mercy on us.*

Heart of Jesus, tabernacle of the Most High, *Have mercy on us.*

Heart of Jesus, house of God and gate of Heaven, *Have mercy on us.*

Heart of Jesus, glowing furnace of charity, *Have mercy on us.*

Heart of Jesus, vessel of justice and love, *Have mercy on us.*

Heart of Jesus, full of goodness and love, *Have mercy on us.*

Heart of Jesus, abyss of all virtues, *Have mercy on us.*

Heart of Jesus, most worthy of all praise, and knowledge, *Have mercy on us.*

Heart of Jesus, wherein dwells all the fullness of the Godhead, *Have mercy on us.*

Heart of Jesus, in Whom the Father is wed,	*Have mercy on us.*
Heart of Jesus, of Whose fullness we have all received,	*Have mercy on us.*
Heart of Jesus, desire of the everlasting hills,	*Have mercy on us.*
Heart of Jesus, patient and rich in mercy,	*Have mercy on us.*
Heart of Jesus, rich unto all who call upon Thee,	*Have mercy on us.*
Heart of Jesus, fount of life and holiness,	*Have mercy on us.*
Heart of Jesus, propitiation for our offenses,	*Have mercy on us.*
Heart of Jesus, overwhelmed with reproaches,	*Have mercy on us.*
Heart of Jesus, bruised for our iniquities,	*Have mercy on us.*
Heart of Jesus, obedient even unto death,	*Have mercy on us.*
Heart of Jesus, pierced with a lance,	*Have mercy on us.*
Heart of Jesus, source of all consolation,	*Have mercy on us.*
Heart of Jesus, our life and resurrection,	*Have mercy on us.*
Heart of Jesus, our peace and reconciliation,	*Have mercy on us.*
Heart of Jesus, victim for our sins,	*Have mercy on us.*

Heart of Jesus, salvation of
those who hope in Thee, *Have mercy on us.*

Heart of Jesus, hope of those
who die in Thee, *Have mercy on us.*

Heart of Jesus, delight of all
Saints, *Have mercy on us.*

Lamb of God, Who takest away
the sins of the world, *Spare us, O Lord.*

Lamb of God, Who takest away
the sins of the world, *Graciously hear us, O Lord.*

Lamb of God, Who takest away
the sins of the world. *Have mercy on us.*

Jesus, meek and humble
of Heart, *Make our hearts like unto Thine.*

Almighty and everlasting God, look upon the Heart of Thy well-beloved Son and upon the praise and satisfaction which He offers unto Thee in the name of sinners; and do Thou of Thy great goodness grant them pardon when they seek Thy mercy, in the name of Thy Son, Jesus Christ, who liveth and reigneth with Thee for ever and ever. Amen.

The Litany of Our Lady of Loreto

L. Lord, have mercy on us.
A. Christ, have mercy on us.

L. Lord, have mercy on us.
Christ, hear us.
A. Christ, graciously hear us.

God the Father of Heaven,	*Have mercy on us.*
God the Son, Redeemer of the world,	*Have mercy on us.*
God the Holy Ghost,	*Have mercy on us.*
Holy Trinity, one God,	*Have mercy on us.*
Holy Mary,	*Pray for us.*
Holy Mother of God,	*Pray for us.*
Holy Virgin of virgins,	*Pray for us.*
Mother of Christ	*Pray for us.*
Mother of divine grace,	*Pray for us.*
Mother most pure,	*Pray for us.*
Mother most chaste,	*Pray for us.*
Mother inviolate,	*Pray for us.*
Mother undefiled,	*Pray for us.*
Mother most amiable,	*Pray for us.*
Mother most admirable,	*Pray for us.*
Mother of good counsel,	*Pray for us.*
Mother of our Creator,	*Pray for us.*

Mother of our Savior,	*Pray for us.*
Virgin most prudent,	*Pray for us.*
Virgin most venerable,	*Pray for us.*
Virgin most renowned,	*Pray for us.*
Virgin most powerful,	*Pray for us.*
Virgin most merciful,	*Pray for us.*
Virgin most faithful,	*Pray for us.*
Mirror of justice,	*Pray for us.*
Seat of wisdom,	*Pray for us.*
Cause of joy,	*Pray for us.*
Spiritual vessel,	*Pray for us.*
Vessel of honor,	*Pray for us.*
Singular vessel of devotion,	*Pray for us.*
Mystical rose,	*Pray for us.*
Tower of David,	*Pray for us.*
Tower of ivory,	*Pray for us.*
House of gold,	*Pray for us.*
Ark of the covenant,	*Pray for us.*
Gate of Heaven,	*Pray for us.*
Morning star,	*Pray for us.*
Health of the sick,	*Pray for us.*
Refuge of sinners,	*Pray for us.*

Comforter of the afflicted,	*Pray for us.*
Help of Christians,	*Pray for us.*
Queen of Angels,	*Pray for us.*
Queen of Patriarchs,	*Pray for us.*
Queen of Prophets,	*Pray for us.*
Queen of Apostles,	*Pray for us.*
Queen of Martyrs,	*Pray for us.*
Queen of Confessors,	*Pray for us.*
Queen of Virgins,	*Pray for us.*
Queen of all Saints,	*Pray for us.*
Queen conceived without original sin,	*Pray for us.*
Queen of the most holy Rosary,	*Pray for us.*
Queen of peace,	*Pray for us.*

Lamb of God, Who takest away
the sins of the world, *Spare us, O Lord.*

Lamb of God, Who takest away
the sins of the world, *Graciously hear us, O Lord.*

Lamb of God, Who takest away
the sins of the world, *Have mercy on us.*

Pray for us, O holy Mother of God, *That we may be made worthy of the promises of Christ.*

Let us pray.

Grant, we beseech Thee, O Lord God, unto us Thy servants, that we may rejoice in continual health of mind and body; and, by the glorious intercession of blessed Mary ever Virgin, may be delivered from present sadness, and enter into the joy of Thine eternal gladness. Through Christ our Lord. Amen.

Litany of St. Joseph

Leader - Lord, have mercy on us.
All - Christ, have mercy on us.

Lord, have mercy on us;
Christ hear us, *Christ, graciously hear us.*

God, the Father of Heaven, *Have mercy on us.*

God, the Son, Redeemer of the world, *Have mercy on us.*

God, the Holy Spirit, *Have mercy on us.*

Holy Trinity, One God, *Have mercy on us.*

Holy Mary, *Pray for us.*

St. Joseph, *Pray for us (or) thank you.*

Renowned offspring of David, *Pray for us (or) thank you.*

Splendor of Patriarchs, *Pray for us (or) thank you.*

Spouse of the Mother of God, *Pray for us (or) thank you.*

Chaste guardian of the Virgin, *Pray for us (or) thank you.*

Foster father of the Son of God, *Pray for us (or) thank you.*

Watchful defender of Christ, *Pray for us (or) thank you.*

Head of the Holy Family,	*Pray for us (or) thank you.*
Joseph most just,	*Pray for us (or) thank you.*
Joseph most pure,	*Pray for us (or) thank you.*
Joseph most prudent,	*Pray for us (or) thank you.*
Joseph most courageous,	*Pray for us (or) thank you.*
Joseph most obedient,	*Pray for us (or) thank you.*
Joseph most faithful,	*Pray for us (or) thank you.*
Mirror of patience,	*Pray for us (or) thank you.*
Lover of poverty,	*Pray for us (or) thank you.*
Model for all who work,	*Pray for us (or) thank you.*
Glory of family life,	*Pray for us (or) thank you.*

Guardian of virgins,	*Pray for us (or) thank you.*
Mainstay of families,	*Pray for us (or) thank you.*
Comfort of the afflicted,	*Pray for us (or) thank you.*
Hope of the sick,	*Pray for us (or) thank you.*
Patron of the dying,	*Pray for us (or) thank you.*
Terror of the demons,	*Pray for us (or) thank you.*
Protector of the Holy Church,	*Pray for us (or) thank you.*
Lamb of God, who takest away the sins of the world,	*Spare us, O Lord.*
Lamb of God, Who takest away the sins of the world,	*Graciously hear us, O Lord.*
Lamb of God, Who takest away the sins of the world,	*Have mercy on us.*
He made him lord over His household.	*And ruler of all His possessions.*

Let us pray

My God, Who in Your unspeakable providence did grant to choose blessed Joseph to be the spouse of Your own most holy Mother, grant we beg You, that we may have him for our mediator in Heaven, whom we venerate as our defender on earth, who lives and reigns world without end. Amen.

Chaplet of the Divine Mercy

In the early 1930's, Sister M. Faustina, of the Congregation of the Sisters of Our Lady of Mercy, was visited by Our Lord and entrusted with a wonderful message of Mercy for all mankind.

"Tell distressed mankind to nestle close to My merciful Heart, and I will fill them with peace ... Mankind will not find peace until it turns with confidence to My Mercy."

Jesus taught her to say this prayer on ordinary rosary beads:

"First say one **'Our Father', 'Hail Mary'** *and* **'I believe'.**

Then on the large beads say the following words:

'Eternal Father, I offer You the Body and Blood, Soul and Divinity of Your dearly beloved Son, Our Lord Jesus Christ, in atonement for our sins and those of the whole world.'

On the smaller beads you are to say the following words:

'For the sake of His sorrowful Passion have mercy on us and on the whole world.'

After the five decades you are to say these words three times:

'Holy God, Holy Mighty One, Holy Immortal One, have mercy on us and on the whole world.' "

Jesus said later to Sister Faustina: "I want the whole world to know My infinite Mercy. I want to give unimaginable graces to those who trust in My Mercy."

Primarily responsible for the resurgence of the devotion to the Divine Mercy was the Archbishop of Sister Faustina's home diocese of Cracow, Poland, Karol Cardinal Wojtyla, now Pope John Paul II.

Jesus, I Trust in You!

Officers and Staff

Jerome F. Coniker
President - Founder
Gwen C. Coniker
Wife, Mother and Writer
Rev. William J. Dorney
Vice President
Dale Francis
Journalist - Program Editor
Rev. John A. Hardon, S.J.
Vice President - Theological Director
Mother Immaculata, H.M.C.
AFC Program Author
William I. Isaacson
Legal Counsel
Rev. Gene Jakubek, S.J.
Television Advisor
Rev. Lawrence G. Lovasik, S.V.D.
AFC Program Author
John R. McGuire
Treasurer
Rev. Thomas A. Morrison, O.P.
Thomistic Advisor
Dr. Thomas A. Prier, M.D.
Secretary - Co-Founder
Dr. Burns K. Seeley, Ph.D.
Vice President - Staff Theologian
Sr. John Vianney, S.S.N.D.
First Suffering Sacri-State Member

Advisory Council

John Joseph Cardinal Carberry, D.D.
Former Archbishop of St. Louis
Mario Luigi Cardinal Ciappi, O.P.
Official Theologian of the Supreme Pontiff
Terence Cardinal Cooke, D.D.
Archbishop of New York & Military Vicar
Humberto Cardinal Medeiros, D.D.
Archbishop of Boston
Silvio Cardinal Oddi, D.D.
Prefect, Sacred Congregation for Priests
Archbishop Augustine P. Mayer, O.S.B.
Secretary, The Sacred Congregation for Religious & Secular Institutes
Bishop Paul Andreotti, O.P.
Bishop of Faisalabad, Pakistan
Bishop Leo J. Brust, D.D.
Vicar General, Archdiocese of Milwaukee
Bishop Thomas J. Welsh, D.D.
Bishop of Arlington
*****Mother Bernadette, H.P.B.**
Handmaids of the Precious Blood
Rev. Gabriel Calvo
Founder of Marriage Encounter
Sister Concetta, D.S.P.
Daughters of St. Paul
Raymond E. Cross
President, Federal Chicago Corp.
Rev. Benedetto D'Amore, O.P.
Editor, Dir., International Center of Studies & Cultural Relations
Dr. Richard A. DeGraff, Ed.D
Educator and Administrator
Rev. John DeMarchi
Mariologist - Missionary
Mother M. Dolorosa, H.P.B.
Handmaids of the Precious Blood
Rev. Francis J. Filas, S.J.
Professor of Theology
John F. Fink
President Our Sunday Visitor
Frank Flick
Founder, Flick-Reedy Corp.

Rev. Robert J. Fox
Pastor, Author, Journalist
Rev. Bernard M. Geiger, O.F.M. Conv.
Nat'l Dir., Knights of Immaculata
W. Doyle Gilligan
President, Lumen Christi Press
Mr. and Mrs. John W. Hand
President, Hand Insurance
Mr. and Mrs. Lowell Hawbaker
Parents of 11 Children
Mrs. Mary Alice Isaacson
Wife, Mother
Rev. Francis J. Kamp, S.V.D.
Treasurer, Divine Word Missionaries
Rev. Msgr. Eugene Kevane
Director, Notre Dame Institute
Rev. Gordon Knese, O.F.M.
Prison Chaplain
*****Rev. Francis Larkin, SS.C.C.**
Founder of our Home Visitation Sacred Heart Program
Rev. Msgr. Paul A. Lenz
Exc. Dir., Bur. of Catholic Indian Missions
Rev. Robert J. McAllister, S.J.
Nat'l Dir., Apostleship of Prayer
Rev. Vincent McCann
Reg'l Superior, Mill Hill Fathers
Mother David Marie, H.P.B.
Mother General
*****August Mauge**
Treasurer - Co-Founder
Mrs. Francis Mauge
Wife
Francis J. Milligan, Jr.
Attorney
Rev. Rodrigo Molina, S.J.
Founder of Lumen Dei
Rev. William G. Most, Ph.D
Theologian, Author, Journalist
Rev. James I. O'Connor, S.J.
Editor, Canon Law Digest
Rev. Gabriel Pausback, O.Carm.
Writer & Former Assistant General
Faustin A. Pipal
Bd. Cham. St. Paul Federal Savings-Chicago
Rev. Msgr. Alphonse Popek
Canon Lawyer and Pastor
Mrs. Thomas A. Prier
Wife and Mother
Rev. Howard Rafferty, O. Carm.
Nat'l Dir., Scapular Center
Rev. Anthony Russo-Alesi, S.J.
Nat'l Dir. of the Boy Savior Youth Movement
John E. Schaeffer
Attorney
Charles F. Scholl
The Dr. Scholl Foundation
William A. Spencer
President, Spencer Bowling Lanes
Mrs. Patricia Spencer
Wife, Mother and Lecturer
Mother Teresa of Calcutta
Foundress of the Missionaries of Charity and our Suffering Sacri-State Member Program
Dr. Paul A. Whelan
Vice President, Parks College of St. Louis University
Mrs. Patricia Whelan
Wife, Mother
Rev. Rinaldo A. Zarlenga, O.P.
Artist

*****Deceased**

Reply Section

1. ( ) Please place this petition at the foot of the altar in your Sacred Hearts Chapel and include it in all of the Masses said for the needs of your petitioners throughout the coming week. Also include these petitions in your vigil of prayer on Fridays, particularly on First Fridays when your president spends his day or night before Our Eucharistic Lord praying for the intentions of all petitions received throughout the month.

_____

_____

_____

_____

_____

_____

_____

_____

_____

2.a ( ) I promise to pray that God will use The Apostolate to inspire people to become an instrument to renew the family and the entire world in Jesus Christ. I would like to be listed as a Sacri-State member and participate in the spiritual benefits of The Apostolate.

2b ( ) I am a priest, and will include the intentions of The Apostolate and all of those who are asking for your prayers in my available Masses, particularly on Fridays.

3. ( ) Enclosed is my best for God, my seed-Charity donation for the vital work of The Apostolate. _____

4. ( ) Enclosed is a list of names of people who should be interested in The Apostolate.

5. ( ) I am not on your mailing list, please add my name.

6. ( ) Please notify me when you start to organize chapters in my area.

7. ( ) I would like to receive more information about Cooperator membership.

8. ( ) Please send your order form for your prayer books and materials.

Please Print:

Name: _____

Address: _____

City & State: _____

Zip: _____

The Apostolate, Box 220, Kenosha, WI 53141

Reply Section

1. ( ) Please place this petition at the foot of the altar in your Sacred Hearts Chapel and include it in all of the Masses said for the needs of your petitioners throughout the coming week. Also include these petitions in your vigil of prayer on Fridays, particularly on First Fridays when your president spends his day or night before Our Eucharistic Lord praying for the intentions of all petitions received throughout the month.

_____

_____

_____

_____

_____

_____

_____

_____

_____

2.a ( ) I promise to pray that God will use The Apostolate to inspire people to become an instrument to renew the family and the entire world in Jesus Christ. I would like to be listed as a Sacri-State member and participate in the spiritual benefits of The Apostolate.

2b ( ) I am a priest, and will include the intentions of The Apostolate and all of those who are asking for your prayers in my available Masses, particularly on Fridays.

3. ( ) Enclosed is my best for God, my seed-Charity donation for the vital work of The Apostolate. _____

4. ( ) Enclosed is a list of names of people who should be interested in The Apostolate.

5. ( ) I am not on your mailing list, please add my name.

6. ( ) Please notify me when you start to organize chapters in my area.

7. ( ) I would like to receive more information about Cooperator membership.

8. ( ) Please send your order form for your prayer books and materials.

Please Print:

Name: _____

Address: _____

City & State: _____

Zip: _____

The Apostolate, Box 220, Kenosha, WI 53141